THE POETIC MANDARIN

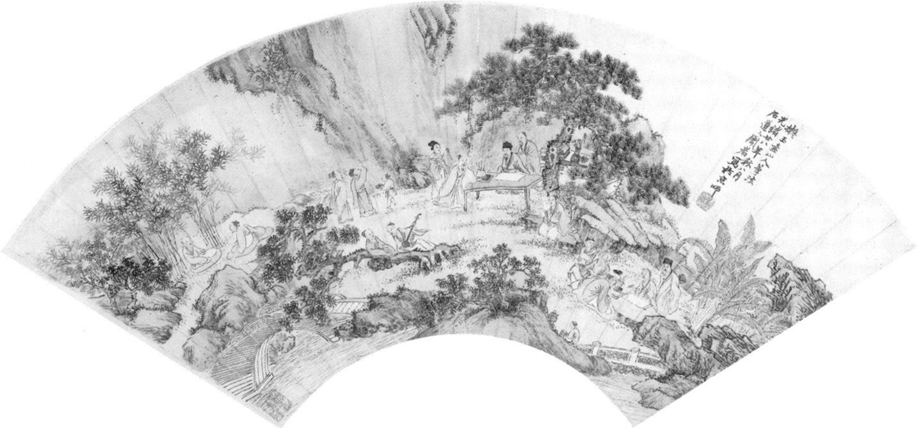

飛流直下
尺疑是銀
天 乙巳四月

For Bill and Amy,
Hoping you enjoy our Catalogue.
With best wishes from James and Mabel,
Alex and Ella.
We still treasure the two framed calligraphies
which you kindly wrote in 1975 for Mabel and
Ella's Father to give to us.

THE POETIC MANDARIN

CHINESE CALLIGRAPHY FROM THE JAMES HAYES COLLECTION

宦海墨韻

許舒藏中國清代書法

Liu Yang

with Edmund Capon and James Hayes

ART GALLERY NSW

Published in association with the exhibition
The poetic mandarin: Chinese calligraphy from the James Hayes collection
23 September – 27 November 2005
Art Gallery of New South Wales
Art Gallery Road, The Domain, Sydney, Australia
www.artgallery.nsw.gov.au

Cataloguing-in-Publication data.

Art Gallery of New South Wales.
The poetic mandarin: Chinese calligraphy from the James Hayes collection = Huan hai mo yun: Xu Shu cang Zhongguo Qing dai shu fa / Liu Yang with Edmund Capon and James Hayes.

Includes bibliography and index.
Text in English with captions, index and title also in Chinese.
ISBN 0 7347 6380 8

1. Hayes, James, 1930– – Art collections – Exhibitions.
2. Art Gallery of New South Wales – Exhibitions. 3. Calligraphy, Chinese – History – 20th century – Exhibitions. 4. Calligraphy, Chinese – History – Ming-Qing dynasties, 1368–1912 – Exhibitions.
I. Liu, Yang, 1961– II. Capon, Edmund. III. Hayes, James, 1930–
IV. T. V. Huan hai mo yun.

Photography Mim Stirling
Editing Lorretta Barnard, Jennifer Blunden
Editorial assistance Natalie Seiz
Design Mark Boxshall
Printing Green & Gold, Sydney

cover: Chen Qikun, *'Zhang Xu's comment on calligraphy' in cursive script* (detail, cat no 7)
page 1: Zhou Yan, *Elegant gathering* 1902. On loan from James Hayes
page 2: Duanfang, *Li Bai's poem in semi-cursive script* 1905 (detail, cat no 29)

The Art Gallery of New South Wales is a statutory body of, and principally funded by, the NSW state government.

Sponsored by

VisAsia

Supported by

Australian Government

Australia-China Council

前史謂筆鋒如徐
美云書貴瘦硬方通
人皆作肥皮饅頭矣
鏡堂仁兄雅屬

FOREWORD

This exhibition and the accompanying publication reveal a very personal journey, albeit one in the public domain. For James Hayes, serving in the Hong Kong government, the art of calligraphy became not only a source of pleasure and satisfaction but also a wonderful insight into the style, manner and machinery of government in late Qing dynasty China. Calligraphy in China fulfils its functional role as the art of writing, conveying meaning and purpose, and as an instrument of government, but there is more to the art and practice of calligraphy. The spirit of the individual lives in the flourish of brush and ink. Calligraphy has thus become the most esteemed of all the arts of China, embracing as it does meaning and expression, the specific and the abstract.

Such qualities and values were sustained in the traditional administrations of dynastic China. The very idea of bureaucrats, mandarins of our modern world, embracing such notions and composing couplets not merely for pleasure but also as demonstrations of the kind of scholarship and learning required of them in their task as administrators, may seem arcane and alien to us but it was a firmly established, and highly valued, tradition of the scholar-official classes in China from the Tang dynasty on. That great tradition is wonderfully illustrated in these scrolls, collected by James Hayes over four decades and now generously donated to the Art Gallery of New South Wales. This exhibition evokes that unique blend of pragmatism and educated imagination which underwrote the ideals of the scholar-official class in dynastic China. It is also an opportunity to recognise a unique contribution to the Asian art collections of our Gallery.

Edmund Capon
Director

Wen Su, *Su Shi's 'comments on calligraphy' in running script* 1938 (detail, cat no 40)

NATURE, POETRY AND THE ART OF CALLIGRAPHY

Edmund Capon

A text on the Chinese art of writing, reputedly written by a famous calligrapher and lute player called Cai Yong (CE 133–192) in the Eastern Han dynasty, begins with the declaration: 'calligraphy began with nature'.[1] Indeed it is not stretching the point to see the flickering images of nature in much calligraphy; a breeze-blown leaf of bamboo is an expressive note of nature just as the flourish of a calligraphic line is an expressive moment of the calligrapher's art. Staccato images of nature's gnarled twigs and branches, leafless in winter, may be echoed in sharp and incisive calligraphic strokes; the arching branch of a supple bamboo stalk reaches like the deft stroke of the master calligrapher's brush and ink; and ripples of water are reflected in the eccentric and straggling lines that linger long after the brush has passed. It is, as Cai Yong suggested, true that the evocative spirit of nature and the elements of the natural world reverberate in the emotive and moving lines of the calligrapher's brush.

Such notions of harmony between nature and the human spirit are familiar themes in Chinese art and calligraphy. Following the demise of the Han dynasty in the early 3rd century, scholars of the so-called Northern and Southern dynasties period (3rd to late 6th centuries), a prolonged period of political disunity and disorder, disenchanted as they were with the world of human affairs, turned to more ethereal matters, to Daoism, Buddhism and indeed to nature, for solace, comfort and inspiration. Lu Ji (261–303) wrote a 'prose poem on literature' in which words derive somehow from nature. This unrhymed piece of prose is full of analogies between the image and spirit of nature and the evocation of the human mind, in words and thus in calligraphy. Take, for example, this excerpt from Lu's prose poem, which addresses the process of creative writing:

At first he withholds his sight and turns his hearing inwards; he is lost in thought, questioning everywhere.
His spirit gallops to the eight ends of the universe, his mind wanders along vast distances.
In the end, as his mood dawns clearer and clearer, objects, now precise in outline, push one another forward.
He sips the essence of letters; he rinses his mouth with the extract of the six arts.[2]
Floating on the heavenly lake, he swims along; plunging into the nether spring, he immerses himself.
Thereupon, submerged words struggle up from the depths, as when a darting fish, hooks in its gills, leaps from a deep lake; as when a high-flying bird drops from a crest of a cloud …

A contemporary of Lu's, Suo Jing (239–303), used images of nature directly to describe calligraphy. In an essay entitled *Caoshu zhuang* (The forces of cursive script) he sought to express the scholars' intent to find certainty and inspiration in nature and thereby drew wonderful allusions in his discourse about *zhuang* (force) and cursive calligraphy:

Cursive script can be smooth as a silver hook,
Or light as a startled bird.
With wings outspread but not yet flying,
As if lifting then settling back …
Like a stallion straining in fury against the bridle,
Or the billowing sea foaming up in breakers,
Like grasses and vines linked together,
With plum trees revealing their splendour,
Like black bears crouching across mountain peaks,
Or swallows chasing one another along water…
A gentle wind brushes through the forest,
Suppressing the grass and fanning the trees …
Crafty black dragons frolic,
And gibbons and squirrels leap.

According to the preface of the *Book of poetry* (*Shi jing* – one of the Six Classics) dating from around the 1st century BCE, good poetry, like good music, possesses a special and uplifting aura, a quality called *feng* (also meaning 'wind') that transforms those who read it. Images of nature were used in poetry as metaphors for morality and political order or indeed as esoteric and highly literate subversions of political order – a tradition that became firmly inscribed into the culture and subtle ways and means of the literati classes of dynastic China. But the symbolism is always there; in the *Book of poetry* the fragrant orchid represents loyalty and friendship and the spiky bramble is a sign of wickedness and treachery. Inevitably the characters written to define these terms carry with them something of their *feng*, their 'aura', thus the image of nature became through expression and symbolism a quality, an essence, of calligraphy.

Calligraphy defines in its meaning and expresses in its brushstrokes. Calligraphy is, therefore, both objective and subjective; Suo Jing again comments on this stating that the artist, the calligrapher, in that moment of making the mark, of flying the brush and ink across the paper, imposes the ego and instinct of self thereby creating, every time, a new form:

There are forms placed high up so they may look down on other forms,
Or in being combined with others, they turn back into themselves.
Some are unrestrained and eccentric,
Others more reflective and conventional.
An eminently talented calligrapher,
In perfecting his art,
Focuses the mind on the fine and the subtle,
Immersing himself in pictographic patterns.
By following both the orthodox and the unorthodox
And by combining forms, he creates new transformations.

Texts and writings on the art of calligraphy, as the pre-eminent form of artistic and intellectual expression, stress not only its universality but also make judgments and establish an order of hierarchy. As early as the Han dynasty, texts were devoted to the rituals and procedures of calligraphy and identified and evaluated the various forms of scripts. At that time the most respected were those of a formal nature, such as large and small seal script, seal-engraving scripts and the all important clerical script, all of which tended, in spite of their clarity and dignity, to lack those qualities of self-expression and personality which subsequently became the hallmark of the great calligraphers. Individuality in the art of writing became recognised in the post-Han Northern and Southern dynasties period. It was then that Suo Jing's point of imbuing the art of writing with the spirit of self, of expression, of personality, that calligraphy acquired an inner strength and meaning inspired by the sense of experience and the response to the world around, that is the natural world.

In the Tang dynasty (618–906) the art of calligraphy became fully recognised as the most powerful and subtle means of personal expression. Among the more enlightening of the influential texts of the time on the mysterious powers of calligraphy was an essay entitled *Jiu shi* (The nine forces). It is said that this text was written some time earlier but it was in the early Tang period that it became something of a mantra in the literati calligraphers' world. It is a text which asserts that the art of writing was a natural as well as an intellectual expression; an extract runs as follows:

> *Calligraphy began with nature. When nature was born, principles of yin and yang were established. When yin and yang were established, forms* [xing] *and forces* [shi] *emerged. By 'hiding the head' and 'protecting the tail'* [of each stroke], *the calligrapher stores power in each character. The action of the brush and the transmitting of force through that action express the beauty and muscle and skin of calligraphy.*

Another illuminating text on the subject, rather pugnaciously titled: *Bizhen tu* (A diagram of the battle formation of the brush) and thought to have been written in the 7th century, also draws wonderful parallels between brushstrokes and elements of nature in describing the spirit of the 'seven brushstrokes':

> Horizontal: *like a cloud formation stretching a thousand li.*
> Dot: *like a stone falling from a high peak.*
> Downward left thrust: *a rhinoceros digging its tusk into the ground.*
> Upward hook: *shooting from a hundred pound crossbow.*
> Vertical stroke: *a withered vine ten thousand years old.*
> Wavelike ending stroke: *a crashing wave or rolling thunder.*
> Left hook: *the sinews and joints of a mighty bow.*

The visual alliterations are both poetic and imaginative but above all they show that calligraphy brushstrokes are manifestly expressions of instinct, spontaneity and naturalness. Even more romantic in its allusions is a text called the *Shu pu* (Manual on calligraphy) written by Sun Guoting in 687:

> *I have seen the wonder of a drop of dew glistening from a dangling needle, a shower of rock hailing down in a raging thunder, a flock of geese gliding in the sky, frantic beasts stampeding in terror, a phoenix dancing, a startled snake slithering away in fright … some brushstrokes are as ominous as gathering clouds, others light as a cicada's wing. When the brush moves forward, a spring bubbles forth; when it stops, the mountains are in repose. Its delicate trace is like a new moon rising on the horizon; its bright residue, like a galaxy of stars across the sky. And though calligraphy is as varied as nature itself and seemingly beyond the powers of man, when the hand is moved by the heart's desire, ingenuity and artistry are united. For the movement of the brush is never arbitrary; it is always purposeful.*

That term 'purposeful' has a certain resonance too, for as we know everything in nature and indeed in the arts of China has its purpose, every stroke, dot and splash in calligraphy has its purpose too, whether it be to properly define the character or to give that added moment of expressive force.

Such pronouncements about the spirit of calligraphy may be arcane but they stress that vital quality that the brushstroke must carry and convey an energy, a spirit that is unique as it is natural. The great Tang poet and calligrapher Huai Su (c735–799) is recorded having said to a colleague:

> *When I see extraordinary mountains in summer clouds, I try to imitate them … good calligraphy resembles a flock of birds darting out from trees, or startled snakes scurrying into the grass …*[3]

During the Tang and Song dynasties, a number of great poet-scholar-calligraphers emerged and set the standards for successive generations, over centuries, to aspire to. They were calligraphers absolutely moved by the spirits, objective and subjective, which brought to their work a majestic fluency, an extraordinary emotive power and a wonderful of subtlety of meaning achieved more through nuance and implication than through specific interpretation. There was, for example, Su Shi, leader of the new literati aesthetic in the 11th century, and his equally talented follower, Huang Tingqian, a Confucian scholar who turned to Daoism, and who saw in his calligraphy a very real expression of natural energy. He wrote of the act of writing as holding back as well as releasing energy – 'of driving each stroke with every force'.[4]

The art of calligraphy in China is far more than the mere act of writing. It is an art of revelation, through meaning, interpretation, emotion, imagination and the sheer physical flourish of the brush and ink.

1 Quoted in Robert Harrist & Wen C Fong: *The embodied image: Chinese calligraphy from the John B Elliot collection*, The Art Museum, University of Princeton 1999, p 34
2 The 'six arts' or *liu yi* of the *Ritual of Zhou*: ceremonies, music, archery, horsemanship, calligraphy and mathematics
3 Harrist & Fong, 1999, pp 45–46
4 Harrist & Fong, 1999, p 48

自然、詩歌與書法藝術

艾德蒙・卡彭

中國漢代的一位書法家蔡邕宣稱，書始于自然。的確，自然的形象在書法中處處可見：在風中搖曳的一片竹葉乃是自然表現性的一個音符，就如一根墨筆線條的揮舞乃是一個書法家藝術表現的靈光一現。正如蔡邕所説的，大自然的精神以及自然世界的元素在書法家筆下那富有感情和運動的線條中找到了回聲。

自然與人的精神之間的和諧是中國藝術和書法的一個熟悉的主題。處于政治動蕩的魏晉南北朝時期的文人，厭倦了塵世的紛擾，轉向佛道與自然，從那兒尋找慰藉和靈感。陸機的《文賦》裏充滿自然形象、精神與人類心靈、詞語及書法之間的類比。例如他說："其始也，皆收視反聽，耽思傍訊。精鶩八極，心遊萬仞。其致也，情曈曨而彌鮮，物昭晰而互進。傾群言之瀝液、漱六藝之芳潤。浮天淵以安流，濯下泉而潛浸。於是沈辭怫悅，若遊魚銜鉤，而出重淵之深；浮藻聯翩，若翰鳥嬰繳，而墜曾雲之峻。"

陸機的同時代人索靖直接運用自然的形象來描繪書法。"蓋草書之爲狀也，婉若銀鉤，漂若驚鸞，舒翼未發，若舉複安 …… 騁驥暴怒逼其轡，海水窊窿揚其波。芝草葡陶還相繼，棠棣融融載其華；玄熊對踞于山嶽，飛燕相追而差池。"

自然的形象在詩歌中常被用作道德、政治秩序的象徵，這是中國士大夫文化中植根很深的一個傳統。例如，在《詩經》中，香蘭被用來表現忠誠和友誼。不可避免地，那些承載象徵意義的字詞也沾上了光彩，通過表現和象徵自然的形象變成了書法的特質，乃至本質。

中國早期有關書法的論述將其視爲藝術與心智表現的卓越形式，並建立起評判優劣的標準。在漢代，缺乏自我表現的篆書和隸書受到重視，因爲文字與禮儀與秩序緊密相關。只有到了後漢時代，個性化的書寫才獲得認可。

到了唐代，書法變成了強有力且又微妙的個人表達的工具。當時有很多論書的文章將筆畫與自然的因素作類比，強調書寫的藝術乃是自然與心智的雙重表達，書法始于自然，它蘊含了自然的力量。這些論述表達出，書法的筆畫乃是本能的，自發性的和自然的表達。

這些論述也說明，書法的筆畫攜帶且表達活力和精神，它們是獨特，自然的。唐宋兩代湧現出一批傑出的書法家，他們爲後人樹立了標準。這些書法家爲靈性所觸動，既客觀又主觀，在其作品中注入了非凡的流暢、感人的力量、以及微妙的意味；而這一切都是通過微妙的體會而非特別的解釋來獲得。

這樣，書法在中國遠遠超越了僅僅是一種書寫的行爲。通過意味、解說、感情、想象以及揮動毛筆，它成爲一種讓人獲得啓示的藝術。[節譯]

THE MANDARIN'S BRUSH: A SOCIAL HISTORY OF CALLIGRAPHIC ART IN LATE IMPERIAL CHINA

Liu Yang

During the Qing dynasty (1644–1912) members of the elite who gained fame for their calligraphy were often equally acclaimed for their achievements in officialdom. This was quite different from other periods in which many calligraphers were retired scholars, noted more for their indifference to official life than for their accomplishments as public figures within various government offices.

Within elite Qing society, calligraphy was admired even more than painting. It was viewed as quintessential yet functional, rather than as merely an independent visual artform or means of self-expression and cultivation. Indeed, among the aspiring upwardly mobile, calligraphy became almost an obsession. More than at any other time, calligraphy became inextricably bound with class and status, the social and the official. Such a phenomenon in late imperial China is unique in the history of calligraphy, and therefore gives rise to new questions for inquiry.

Early studies on the role of Chinese calligraphy focused on format, script type or style, or on the relationship between meaning and form. Missing from these early discourses is any systematic discussion related to the social dimension of calligraphy, particularly in late imperial China: how calligraphy was embedded in politics, work, leisure and the complex web of social obligation that underpinned everyday official and cultural life. This essay is therefore an inquiry into the social history of Chinese calligraphic art.

It was not new in imperial China that social and political processes were to shape artistic preference. Like other forms of art, calligraphy had been closely associated with political power throughout China's history. However, Qing calligraphic art possessed a political dimension of unprecedented scale.

The early Qing dynasty owed its success to three extraordinary emperors who ruled in succession from 1654 to 1796. All three were learned in Chinese culture, and fervent lovers of calligraphy. The first was Kangxi, in power for 61 years. During his rule, he sponsored several ambitious literary projects. He favoured a few ranking mandarins, all of whom excelled in calligraphy. Fang Bao 方苞, a courtier of this reign who served as a vice minister in the Ministry of Ceremonies observed:

> *Whenever the emperor needed to compose calligraphy, such as script for stele, or maxims decorating screens or the throne, he would summon Shen Quan* 沈荃 [a reader of the Hanlin Academy] *to do it. Sometimes he did calligraphy in large scale and asked Shen to inscribe a colophon. Once he asked Shen to make a fair copy of Mi Fu's* [1051–1107] *calligraphy. When he saw that Shen's brush tip was no longer sharp, he got out a new brush and sucked its tip himself in order to soften it. Accompanying the emperor's practice of calligraphy, Shen would touch the weaknesses of Kangxi's script with a delicate hand, and analyse the reason. The emperor was delighted with his loyalty. The gifts he bestowed on Shen, such as royal brushes, clothes and other souvenirs, were countless. People felt honoured to get Shen's calligraphy.*[1]

Kangxi's son, the Yongzheng emperor, reigned briefly (r1723–35) but accomplished much, especially in strengthening the powers of the monarchy. While still young, he already excelled in calligraphy. An anecdote relates that when he was a prince, he once travelled to Hangzhou incognito, where he encountered a poor young scholar selling his own calligraphy. Admiring this man's excellent calligraphy and mastery of *bafa* 八法 (eight methods of brushstrokes), the prince generously contributed a few pieces of gold and urged the young scholar to take part in the civil service exam.[2] Yongzheng's recognition of this man's skill equates with his own – from an aesthetic point of view, Yongzheng may be considered the best calligrapher among these three extraordinary emperors.

The Qianlong emperor, who reigned from 1736 to 1796, combined his father's authoritarianism with his grandfather's support of culture. He practised calligraphy, reviewed and commented on thousands of works of art, oversaw a revised edition of the existing Chinese literature, and composed some 44 000 poems in his lifetime, all written in his characteristic calligraphy. Qianlong also favoured courtiers who excelled in calligraphy. Wang Youdun 汪由敦 (1692–1758), a *jinshi* 進士 (the degree for the highest civil service examination) of Yongzheng's reign, for instance, was promoted to minister of the Council of State, a promotion some scholars of the Qing dynasty believed was mainly due to the emperor's appreciation of his brilliant calligraphy.[3]

When the minority Manchu came to power, a major consideration must have been to consolidate significant cultural materials and integrate them with political expediency. So a policy of placing emphasis on calligraphy, a refined form of cultural communication, would hence serve as a means to culturally unify and legitimise Qing rule. Furthermore the declaration of a calligraphic tradition that can be traced back to Wang Xizhi (act 320–60), recognised by previous dynasties as the foremost example of Chinese calligraphic style, could also help strengthen the Manchu's political legitimacy by identifying the court with scholarly orthodoxy. Such activities could also help win over Chinese intellectuals, who were necessary in running the bureaucracy. The court's influence on calligraphy was then imposed through various means, for example by the frequent conferral of the emperor's own calligraphy onto disciplined mandarins, moral scholars, and model citizens. Wang Shizhen, who served as a *xingzou* 行走 (or 'do duty') at Kangxi's study Nanshufang 南書房, had recorded many such instances in his writings.[4] Exhibiting inscriptions by the emperor across the nation effectively underscored his presence and helped build up a personal cult. They offered a special channel of communication from ruler to his people, while also encouraging emulation following the imperially favoured style.

MEASURE OF A MANDARIN

Placing a premium on the command of literature, history and, more specifically, calligraphy, the civil service examination system had marked effects on the history of calligraphy. The tendency of stressing a candidate's exceptional ability in calligraphy might have already begun in the very early part of the Qing dynasty, where in order to ensure objectivity in evaluation, examination papers were identified by number rather than name. However, according to an anecdote, in 1655 Emperor Shunzhi 'who was paying enthusiastic attention to the literary activities' awarded the *zhuangyuan* 狀元 (the crowning honour in the *jinshi* exam) to the third candidate on the preliminary list selected by examiners because he recognised the contender's handwriting and favoured his calligraphy.[5]

More and more, excellence in calligraphy became a prerequisite to holding high government office. Numerous *biji* 筆記 (miscellaneous notes which took the form of recollections about official and court life) written by scholar-officials in the Qing period make mention of the trends in calligraphy under discussion here. These literary records also offer other insights into the psyche and cultural state of the times.

A late Qing scholar-official Zhu Pengshou, who gained the *jinshi* degree during Guangxu's reign concluded that, 'Every year in the metropolitan examination from among the 300 to 400 *jinshi* degree recipients, of those who stood out to obtain the highest honours, some achieved it by right of their literary fame; others excelled in calligraphy. The conjecture that they would win the title was not a surprising probability'.[6] His comments were based on a great many literary accounts, often from the authors' first-hand experiences. For instance Wan Shizhen, a *jinshi* of 1685 and once the minister of Punishments, gives the account:

> *Years ago, when I lived at the capital, in the year* bingchen [1676] … *a young man, Zhan Xiaoyi from Changshu, who had just failed contending for the* jinshi *exam, often came to visit me and showed me his poems, pleading for advice. I said to him, 'Your calligraphy is excellent, and your poem does not have any sentiment of plainness or haggardness. You will definitely obtain the* zhuangyuan *title in future.' In the year of* jiwei [1679], *just as one would expect, he succeeded in the examination with the highest honour.*[7]

The expectation could be self-imposed, such as Feng Wenwei, a candidate in 1876 from Zhejiang who was so proud of his calligraphy (regarded as 'resembling a beautiful lady wearing a flower') that he had considered himself the only contender for the highest honour. He was extremely disappointed when Cao Zhongming from Weixian, Shandong province, was announced the *zhuangyuan*. However, when the exam papers were exhibited publicly, Feng was dazzled by the marvellous strength of Cao's calligraphy and conceded that the award was justly won.[8]

It became an open secret that government employees with experience in the clerical work of different ministries would have a better chance than others at the exam because of their familiarity with the imperial taste in calligraphy. A late Qing writer He Shensheng tells us that the brightest *jinshi* candidates often stood out from those who served as *zhangjing* 章京 (secretaries) at Junjichu (the Council of State). Bi Yuan 畢沅 (in 1760), Huang Siyong 黃思永 (1880) and Wu Lu 吳魯 (1890), who were awarded the highest honours, and Zhu Chongguang 諸重光 (1760) and Zhao Yi 趙翼 (1761) who received second and third highest honours respectively, were just a few examples.[9]

In the later Qing period, the emphasis on calligraphy was even stricter: 'Since Jiaqing and Daoguang, the metropolitan exam was inclined to lay stress on the method of regular script … After Jiaqing and Daoguang, in the court exam value was especially placed upon the script style'.[10] The early 19th-century scholar Luo Dunrong criticised such practices of the Daoguang period by saying, 'The examiners laid particular attention to the calligraphy, even excusing the content of an essay. Such is merely an interest in the skill of a typist or secretary. [For a contender] a minor mistake in writing could result in a failure to become a member of the Hanlin Academy, therefore leaving lifelong regrets'.[11] In reality, there were many such 'lifelong regrets': of Gong

Zizhen 龔自珍 (1792–1841), poet, scholar and one of the most influential figures in late Qing thought, it was said, 'in all his life he was not good at calligraphy; as a consequence he has never had a chance to get into the Hanlin Academy'. According to an anecdote, he felt so humiliated that he required his daughters, daughters-in-law, concubines and maidservants all to learn the *guan'geti* 館閣體 style necessary for the civil service exam. Whenever a guest turned the topic to the Hanlin, he would sneer by saying, 'What of today's Hanlin is worth mentioning anyway? Every woman in my family could enter the Hanlin given that they all excel in calligraphy'.[12]

Occasionally exceptions were made for unusual cases. According to Niu Xiu, selected as a student at the Guozijian Imperial Academy in 1672, the calligraphy of Li Pan 李蟠, *zhuangyuan* of the year 1697, was not first-rate. On the day of the metropolitan exam, when by nightfall all other contenders had left, only Li was still working on his paper, and finished just before midnight. When this was reported to the emperor, he appreciated and admired Li's painstaking efforts and conferred on him the highest honour.[13] Prince Zhaolian (1770–?) recounts that Wang Tingzhen 汪廷珍 (1757–1827), later assistant grand secretary in 1825, 'had never achieved excellence in calligraphy. At the court exam of 1789, [the chief examiner] Peng Yuanrui彭元瑞 [1731–1803, assistant grand secretary at the time] recommended he be awarded the second highest honour, due to his keen insight and judgment. This rarely happened in recent examinations'.[14] In 1895 the whole country was immersed in the grief and indignation of losing a naval battle against the Japanese, and the consequent humiliating treaty. Emperor Dezong conferred the highest honour to Luo Chengxiang 駱成驤, the number nine candidate on the preliminary list, for his deep feeling of grief and discernment over the current political affair. The late Qing writer He Shengsheng commented, 'Since Jiaqing and Daoguang, the metropolitan exam lay particular stress on calligraphy. Luo was not good at it, yet was chosen as *zhuangyuan*; such was truly an act that broke the rule'.[15]

Mastering calligraphy not only improved one's chance of achieving higher honours in the *jinshi* examination but also created broader opportunities for entering government service and gaining promotion. In 1705 for instance, during his fifth southern inspection trip, Kangxi decreed a number of scholars from the areas of Zhejiang and Jiangsu who passed the county or provincial level exam and excelled in calligraphy, to attend to the clerical works in the inner court.[16] Qian Yong (1759–1844), a native of Henan who excelled in calligraphy, recalls that while Jiang Sheng 姜晟 (later deputy minister within the Ministry of Punishments) was still the governor of Hunan, by chance he saw Qian's calligraphic work. It inspired such admirable sentiment that he immediately dispatched an official to Qian's home to invite him to take up a position in his administration.[17]

Brilliant hands in calligraphy were in high demand. According to Ouyang Zhaoxiong and Jin Anqing, two scholars from the Daoguang and Xianfeng periods (1821–60):

When officialdom was still in a stable situation, from upper class to lower class, everyone laid special attention on calligraphy ... some officials employed dozens of young men who excelled in calligraphy. By the time the regular script was fashionable, the so-called 'foundation of Ou, surface of Zhao' [meaning a combination of the two styles of Ouyang Xun of Tang and Zhao Mengfu of Yuan, see cat no 4], *was all magnificent yet solid; dozens of calligraphers exhibit a unique style, as if from one hand. If there were long documents, several people would work in collaboration. When finally sections were put together, one could not tell they were done by different hands.*[18]

Since employees who attended to clerical works were often required in the capital, and calligraphy was a prerequisite for holding such posts, a distinct career emerged for those willing to sit an examination in place of another person. Many 'substitute examinees' were candidates who temporarily stayed in the capital waiting to take the metropolitan *jinshi* exam (held every three years). The commission cost between ten and a hundred pieces of gold ('一百金'), depending on the substitute examinee's level of fame. In the year 1883, a certain Ma Xinglian from Zhejiang province, was extremely well known for his exceptional *kaishu* (regular script). Hiring him as a substitute guaranteed a position in the first three places, though the cost for gaining the highest honour was expensive: 800 pieces of gold.[19]

Often, the preference for calligraphy over an applicant's other skills failed to select appropriate candidates to fill government posts. The disadvantage of such practice gradually became obvious, especially during the late Qing, when China entered a period of turmoil. Many scholar-officials may have excelled in calligraphy but were unsuited to the task of arresting the steady decline of the empire. Without political acumen and strategy, they could not save the empire from collapsing under its own cultural senility, economic breakdown and military impotency. In a crumbling 19th-century empire, the system of selecting public servants weighted on narrow visual or aesthetic regulations rather than intellect could result in disaster. Some bureaucrats holding office through such a system were blind to any alternative political structure. In a way, the system contributed to the decline not only of calligraphy but also of its very social foundations.

Some men of insight recognised the folly of such a system. In the first year of Xianfeng (1851) a court censor, Wang Maoyin 王茂蔭, presented a memorial to the emperor suggesting:

In the metropolitan exam and in the promotional exam afterwards [chaokao '朝考'], *importance should be attached to content. From now on, your majesty should decree that examiners must choose essays with outstanding wisdom to present to the throne for final decision. Therefore letting everyone know that what the court weighted was the content, not the calligraphy.*[20]

Two years later, when the southern capital Nanjing fell into the Taiping Tianguo rebels' hands, public opinion began to blame local governors such as Lu Jianying 陸建瀛, the governor-general of Liangjiang provinces. However a scholar-official Chen Kangqi, who once held the position of second-class secretary in the Ministry of Punishments during the Xianfeng period, commented that scholar-officials such as those condemned by public opinion had entered into official careers chiefly through their excellent command of calligraphy ('本以試帖楷書進身'). But lacking any political judgment or military capability, it is not surprising that they would push the panic button in face of danger.[21] Another author of same period also mentions that 'Recent memorials presented to the throne all ridiculed the way of selecting public servants, considering it should not specially pay attention to the *xiaokai* 小楷 [lesser regular script] used in the exam'.[22] Such views suggest that criticism of the system at the very end of the Qing dynasty was quite strong.

SHIFTING COURTLY TASTES

Wang Shizhen writes in one of his *biji* (miscellaneous notes):

> *In this dynasty, a* zhuangyuan *would have to be selected from those who excelled in calligraphy. In Shunzhi's reign, because the throne favoured the style of Ouyang Xun, therefore Zou Zhongyi* 鄒忠倚 *and Sun Cheng'en* 孫承恩, *who followed the Ouyang style were awarded the highest honours in 1652 and 1718 respectively. Emperor Kangxi had a predilection for calligraphy of the two Wangs* [Wang Xizhi and his son Wang Xianzhi], *therefore those who received the highest honours in* jinshi *exam all followed the calligraphic models of* Huangting jing 黃庭經 *and* Le Yi lun 樂毅論, *both by Wang Xizhi. The examples include Gui Yunsu* 歸允肅 *in 1679, Cai Shengyuan* 蔡升元 *in 1682, and Wang Yi* 汪繹 *in 1700.*[23]

Wang's account is testimony to the dominance of the emperor's changing calligraphic taste in the selection of *jinshi* candidates, which would consequently exercise a great impact on the calligraphy style in vogue. Scholars who cherished hopes of passing the civil service exam and mandarins who worked under such circumstances were all forced to adapt to current imperial taste. Thus the early part of the Qing dynasty is associated with the cursive and running scripts, with a primary emphasis on their lineage traced back to Dong Qichang (1555–1636), Zhao Mengfu (1254–1322) and eventually to Wang Xizhi of 4th century.

Kangxi took Dong Qichang's calligraphy as the model for his own writing. The emperor doted upon the courtiers who excelled in Dong's style. One such courtier was Gao Shiqi (1645–1704), a native of Hangzhou, who had never gained any high-degree in the civil service examination. He had the honour to serve at the emperor's

Southern Study purely because of his excellent calligraphy in Dong's style. When he was later impeached by court censors for corruption, he was merely dismissed by the emperor instead of criminally charged.

While throughout the Kangxi period educated individuals primarily practised calligraphy in the style of Dong Qichang, the emperor Qianlong esteemed the calligraphy of Zhao Mengfu and imitated his hand. Under Qianlong's influence, 'Dong Qichang bade farewell, Zhao Mengfu rose instead and his calligraphy was treasured'.[24]

Both Dong's and Zhao's styles were for the most part natural and unrestrained, elegant and refined. However, they were considered lacking in strength and vigour. Because the style of the great Tang calligrapher Yan Zhenqing (709–85) was bold and vigorous, showing spaciousness and breadth, it therefore became the fashion during emperors Yongzheng and Qianlong's reigns to take Yan's calligraphy as a model for foundation of practice. Having mastered this, the elegant styles of Dong and Zhao were then followed. This was called 'foundation of Yan, surface of Zhao [or Dong] 顏體趙面'.

Imperial taste continued to dominate calligraphic aesthetic in the late Qing. A mandarin Li Jun (?–1859), who served as a deputy minister within the Ministry of Punishments, described the trend: 'During Daoguang's reign, Liu Gongquan's calligraphy was very popular. The Hanlin Academy was teased as the "Yamen of Willow" [the surname 'Liu' also means 'willow'] 柳衙, the Imperial Study as the "Study of Serene Willow 深柳讀書堂", and the Qingmitang Hall at Hanlin Academy as "Ten-thousand-Willow Hall".'[25]

However imperial taste for certain styles of calligraphy resulted in a court calligraphic style that contrasted with the free and spontaneous manner of the individual's brushwork, and the forms of calligraphy championed by the court became increasingly conventionalised and stagnant. Such disadvantage is reflected in a script style known as *guan'geti* 館閣體 (style of cabinet), commonly used by contenders at the civil service examination.

The *guan'geti* style can be considered a derivation of the *kaishu* (regular script) type, yet stiffer and more tightly knit (one can catch a glimpse of such style of script from cat nos 38, 46). It is characterised by greater uniformity in the way individual characters are constructed, resulting in highly regular forms. The script stressed the spatial integrity of characters within columns. It is comparable to the Buddhist sutra style, and in its extreme almost looks like printed fonts. Throughout the Qing dynasty, *guan'geti* became an exacting 'chancellery style' that was not only a must for all students who aspired to government office, but a model for all government documents. The style became an orthodox school, and the calligraphy an art with brushwork as intricate as the bureaucratic system. The following remark by two scholars of the Xianfeng period demonstrate how *guan'geti* evolved in response to imperial taste:

The guan'geti *style changes as time moves, yet such changes were all made through observing the ruler's idea. At the beginning of this dynasty, the emperor favoured the Dong Qichang's calligraphy, and scholar-officials all followed suit. Of this style, the most famous calligraphers were Zha Shengshan 查聲山 and Jiang Ximing 姜西溟. When it came to the period of Yongzheng and Qianlong, the imperial taste shifted to a style that took Yan Zhengqing as the foundation yet absorbed elements of Zhao Menfu and Mi Fu, what is commonly known as being 'black, smooth, foursquare and bright.' The spirit of good fortune this style reflected is quite imposing. In the Jiaqing period, the calligraphic taste is changed to the Ouyang Xun style, and the Prince Cheng was the initiator. During Daoguang's reign, Liu Gongquan's script became prevalent, calligraphers such as Qi Shouyang 祁壽陽, were considered the best. Since Xianfeng's reign, the mainstream taste came to favour a style that was either Ouyang Xun, Liu Gongquan or Yan Zhengqing.*[26]

WEBS OF OBLIGATION

Today, to appreciate the beauty of Chinese calligraphy, one does not have to know how to read Chinese characters. For the scholar-officials of late imperial China, however, the art of calligraphy was primarily an instrument of bureaucracy and communication. Yet from written memorials presented to the throne, daily documentation and correspondence to simple notes, shop signs, and inscriptions on tablets and gateways at famous sites (ancestral or other religious temples and scenic spots), when written well, all such things roused the aesthetic response of those who saw them. As such they lingered with joy in the minds of the viewers, who savoured the attractiveness and power of the calligraphy.

Within the bureaucracy, a basic requirement for a mandarin was the practice of routine calligraphy, including the preparation of memorials to be presented to the emperor. Yet in addition to its content, the quality of a bureaucrat's calligraphy might change the course of his career. According to Zhu Guozhen of the early 17th century, who held the post of minister of the Civil Office in the late Ming dynasty, 'When officials in former days presented a memorial to the throne, they were required to write it with their own hand; this custom was retained unchanged from the Song dynasty. It was interrupted in the Yuan period'.[27] The Ming resumed the tradition. Personal handwriting was said to reflect an official's reverence and sincere intention to the court. Zhu Guozhen gave a Ming dynasty example of how the throne's appreciation of such intention could change an official's prospects: Hu Zongxian 胡宗憲 (?–1565), the minister of war and concurrent governor for the Resistance Against Japanese Pirates, was impeached for improper conduct in office and put in prison. The emperor Jiajing (r1522–66) deeply sympathised with him, not only because of his accomplishments in defending the dynasty during the rebellion but also because he always wrote memorials in his own hand. These exposed his respectful and sincere sentiments towards the court, proving that he was a person of forthright, bold and unconstrained character.

Such tradition was carried on in the Qing. One learns from the writings of Xu Xiling and Qian Yong (1759–1844) that Zhang Dayou 張大有, the director-general for grain transportation during Emperor Yongzheng's reign, once presented a memorial to the emperor, pleading for the throne to allow him to ask an assistant to write the memorial instead, as his own hand kept shivering. The emperor replied: 'The allograph may be allowed if you sustain many activities; though you are still required to write a secret memorial. It does not matter much even if the characters are crassly brushed, or tend to slight running or cursive strokes. Nothing more is needed than to convey ideas clearly. Loyalty does not reflect in this'.[28] The author mentioned that Sun Shiyi 孫士毅, then the governor of Liangguang province, also got the same reply from the throne. The author's comment, 'Our Majesty is so lenient and enlightened in treating courtiers', implies that, during other periods, the requirement for handwriting would have been sterner.

The role the elite played in late imperial China is probably without parallel in other cultures. Combining the roles of mandarin, scholar, calligrapher and sometimes painter, poet and philosopher, they wrote numerous calligraphies for specific occasions and recipients to fulfil various social obligations.

One such social obligation was to write titles, eulogies or couplets (carved on tablets) for ancestral temples. In China, ancestral worship which emphasises the influence of deceased relatives on the living is at the core of common religious practice. Temples or shrines formed a centre for religious activities, and helped preserve a strong sense of familial or clan solidarity. It would be a great honour for a family or clan to have calligraphy by an esteemed mandarin-scholar – or even the ruler – hung in their ancestral shrine. A great number of calligraphic works decorating such shrines by calligraphers in this exhibition are still seen in China, especially in Guangdong province. The following examples are just a few of them.

The ancestral shrine of the He family in a village called Yanqiaocun, Jiujiang, Foshan, for instance, was rebuilt in 1814 by He Wenqi 何文綺, who served as second-class assistant secretary in the Ministry of War in the early Jiaqing period but later retired to Guangzhou to teach. Inside the main hall, above the altar, a tablet bearing the three characters Bojutang 播聚堂 (Hall of Sowing and Assembling) were brushed by Li Wentian (cat no 19) in 1892. The title on the front gate 'Six-generation ancestral shrine of He clan 何氏六世祖祠' was written by Liang Liuzao 梁騮藻 (*juren* in 1867). Outside, an inscription carved on the memorial stele was written by Zhang Zhidong (cat no 21) who was then the governor of Liangguang. The Li Wentian family shrine at Shangcun village in Shunde, in turn, has two wooden tablets bearing characters *longhu* 龍虎 (dragon and tiger) and *fushou* 福壽 (fortune and longevity) respectively.

They were from the hand of Empress Dowager Cixi and were conferred to Li in 1864.

Another closely related social obligation for scholar-officials was to write epitaphs and memorial stele for their peers or other esteemed persons. In a well-known article composed by the Song dynasty writer Zeng Gong (1019–83), the author criticised the then current practice of epitaph writing with exaggerated praise unworthy of the recipient. He considered that only those who 'contemplated lofty morals' and were writers 'of proficiency' deserved an epitaph (see cat no 31). The article demonstrates a widespread practice in funereal art in medieval China, a situation retained unaltered in the Qing dynasty.

In 1888 a villager named Qi Zhankui from Dong'an in Zhili (in modern Hebei) vowed at a Buddhist pagoda that if his dying mother recovered, he would sacrifice his own young life. When his wish was granted, he jumped from the summit of the pagoda and died. The throne decided to honour Qi's moral of filial piety, and ordered a stele with an inscription brushed by Li Wentian to be erected in his memory next to the pagoda.[29]

Zhang Zhidong's epitaph in his hometown of Nanpi, Hebei, was composed by Chen Baochen 陳寶琛, mentor of the last Qing dynasty emperor Puyi. The calligraphy in seal script on the epitaph's lid was by Xu Shichang (cat no 24). The tomb and shrine of Han Yu (768–824), one of the Tang dynasty's most influential poets and officials, in Mengzhou, Henan province, now has a stele inscribed by Feng Mingchang (cat no 3) from 1789 (a substitute of the original one established in Tang dynasty). The inscription on Feng Mingchang's tomb stele, in Dasi, Qinbei, Guangxi province, in turn was done by his mentor Weng Fanggang (1733–1818), the grand secretary and an esteemed scholar.

A couplet seen in the Shrine of the Revered Mr Tie 鐵公祠, located in Daming Lake, Nanjing, was composed by Zhang Zhiwan (cat no 10) in praise of Tie Xuan 鐵鉉, the loyal Ming dynasty general who died while fighting against the dissident prince Zhu Di in 1402. The Shi Kefa Shrine in Yangzhou, Jiangsu province, was built in the Qing dynasty in memory of this loyal general who led the resistance against the Manchu army at the very end of the Ming Dynasty. On the sidewall of the veranda, a great number of calligraphies carved on slabs were inserted into the wall. These were writings in praise of this hero by many of the scholar-officials of the Qing dynasty, including Liu Yong (see cat no 28) and others.

It has almost been an unwritten rule in China that esteemed calligraphers write signs for shops, a custom still in practice even today. Wandering though the streets, one feels as if they are visiting a calligraphy gallery. Hanwenzhai 翰文齋 in Beijing was one of the oldest bookstores at Liulichang area, opened around the late 1870s. The shop's sign was made by Li Wentian during one of his irregular visits to the store during Guangxu period.[30] Today, one can still see sign for Xinghualou 杏花樓 (Pavilion of Apricot Blossoms), a famous restaurant in Guangzhou, written by Zhu Ruzhen (cat no 35) in 1930 in regular script. A no longer existing restaurant *Qihonglu* 憩虹廬 (Hut of a Resting Rainbow) in Shanghai was established by the relatives of Li Zhanzhi (cat no 34). The restaurant's name and sign were made after Li's style name by Wang Shoupeng 王壽彭, *zhuangyuan* of the year 1903 when Li received his *jinshi* degree.

In 1669 Wang Zhihe, a *juren* from Anhui, failed in the metropolitan examination. He wanted to return to his hometown, but short of travelling expenses decided to stay in Beijing till the next examination. To support himself he took on his family's business of making bean curd, and also created a new type of product: 'smelly tofu'. After many unsuccessful attempts at passing the examination, he eventually gave up his dream of officialdom and opened a 'smelly tofu' shop in 1678. The shop gained such a reputation that during the late Qing, even Empress Dowager Cixi favoured its smelly tofu and demanded it every day. Because of the imperial preference, the business thrived. The shop's name, Wang Zhihe Catsup Shop 王致和南醬園, was written on two wooden boards by 1868's *zhuangyuan* Sun Jiading 孫家鼎 and *jinshi* Lu Qiguang (cat no 17). The boards were decorated with dragons indicating imperial preference. Sun also composed two pairs of couplets mounted on the shop entrance.

Mandarins also created calligraphy for favourite scenic spots, although on these occasions more for their own pleasure than at the request of others. Their poetic phrases in handsome calligraphy were not only decorative, they were themselves part of a fascinating scene. One of the best examples occurs in Qixingyan (Rock of the Big Dipper) located in the northern outskirts of Zhaoqing in Guangdong province. A summer resort with lakes, rocks and caves, it has both the charm of Guilin's mountains and the placid beauty of Hangzhou's West Lake. Since the Jin dynasty (265–420), a great number of scholar-officials have inscribed the walls of the caves with poems which eulogise the fascinating beauty of the place. Over 500 of these inscriptions still exist, including some 117 works from the Qing period – one of them by Feng Minchang (cat no 3).

Many of the scholar-offcials in this exhibition left behind calligraphic works at various scenic spots. At the top of the southern sacred mountain, Hengshan, is an inscription *wangritai* 望日台 (platform of beholding the sun) brushed and carved by Feng Minchang in 1791 at the spot where the sunrise can be viewed. Penglai at Yantai, Shandong province, boasts having many historical and scenic sites; it is also regarded as the holy ground of Chinese calligraphy. Among numerous inscriptions, there is one, 'pure wind above blue sea 碧海清風' by Lu Qiguang (cat no 17). Xu Qi (cat no 26), who grew up in a scholar-official's family in Hangzhou, had served the provincial director of education in Guangdong. His graceful calligraphy is seen in many public places in Guangdong and Hangzhou – more than ten of them are at Western Lake. One example is at a Buddhist temple site called Longqiutan in Lianzhou, Guangdong, where his huge running script version of a poem by Tang poet Han Yu is carved on the side of a cliff.

As many scenic spots are closely associated with religious monasteries, these buildings are also home to much scholar-official calligraphy. The couplet in this exhibition – 'The floating life resembles a dream; who is not a sojourner? Thus everywhere would be home if one could settle' (cat no 47) – is one of the most popular couplets at Buddhist temples. The one seen at Ziguosi Temple 資國寺in Fuding, Fujian province, accordingly was composed by '孫將鳴', an unidentified grand secretary (equivalent to prime minister) of the Qing dynasty. The same temple also has a couplet ('Pure fragrance fills the room while the Buddha is in Nirvana; when the bright moon leaps out of the sea the sky becomes higher 清香滿室佛入定, 明月出海天爲高') by Wang Pengshou, *zhuangyuan* of 1903. A wooden tablet bearing four characters *nanhai changchun* 南海長春 (spring forever in the southern sea) written by Zeng Guoquan (cat no 16) in 1857, still hangs at Yunmengsi Temple in Xiangxiang, Hunan province. A lengthy couplet at Hualinsi Temple in Guangzhou was written by Chen Qikun (cat no 7), while at the Dakuige pagoda 大魁閣塔, built at Dalingcun village in Shilouzhen, Panyu, in 1884, a four-character inscription carved on the top of the main gate was written by Li Wentian in 1884: 'strengthening the mount of Bodhi 作鎮菩山'.

BRIDGING MIND AND CULTURE

In dynastic China, a mandarin's moral character was also judged by his closeness to people under his authority. Calligraphy could be used by some officials as a channel for communication, a means of winning their confidence. According to a late 18th-century writer Li Dou, couplets of squire families in Yangzhou were mostly from the hand of Wang Shu 王澍, a second-class secretary in the Ministry of Civil Office.[31] Another account in the same book relates:

> *Gao Chengjue 高承爵, the governor of Yangzhou, excelled in calligraphy. His people loved him, and at the end of the year, they would come to him to request the character* fu *or 'good fortune', and took it as an auspicious gift. Once one of these folk who had already received a* fu *character waited for him outside his official residence, and pleaded for him to rewrite the same character. Gao looked at the one he did and said, 'Sorry, when I did this, the brush was not good.' Such has become a story passed on with approval.*[32]

In some instances, calligraphy enabled bureaucrats to maintain a unifying social bond that transcended factional conflict, lubricating affiliations between incompatible people. How such calligraphic interactions worked in the Qing bureaucracy is demonstrated in the following story. In 1857, there was disharmony between Zeng Guofan (elder brother of Zeng Guoquan, cat no 16) and Zuo Zongtang (cat no 11) because Zuo had criticised Zeng for rushing home for the funeral of his mother during a military campaign. A year later, when they joined together for another military operation, Zuo wrote in his famous seal script a couplet for Zeng at his request, and so the friendship between the two was resumed.[33] In this case, calligraphy formed a bridge between the two arrogant generals.

During the Qing period, the calligraphy produced by well-known scholar-official enjoyed an international reputation. Such was the case of Liang Tongshu 梁同書 (1723–1815), a sub-expositor of the Hanlin Academy of the Qianlong period. According to Qian Yong (1759–1844), 'people requesting his works came following one another's heels. Some even came afar from Japan, Ryukyu, and Korea; all felt happy if they could get a piece of his writing'.[34] Calligraphy also served as an effective means of cultural communication, used by some scholar-officials to strengthen their ties to the hosts of foreign countries and to provoke a sense of pride in their own culture or nation. Li Dou mentions another incident in his book:

> *Wang Ji 汪楫, a native of Jiangdu, could write brilliant calligraphy loaded with spiritual resonance … When he served as an ambassador to Ryukyu* [in 1682], *he was invited to compose a piece of calligraphy to decorate the palatial hall. He swept the brush over the paper with strength and created large works, which dazzled the King who admired him, as if he was assisted by spirits.*[35]

In 1882 a courtier, Ma Jianzhong, served as special envoy to Korea, negotiating this neighbouring country's treaties with the West. Ma recalls that, when the mission was accomplished and the delegation about to depart, there was a farewell party on a Chinese ship: not wine but calligraphy was served on the occasion. Chinese and Korean mandarins took turns to compose calligraphy as presents for each other. The calligraphy of two Korean senior officials was described as 'following Zhao Mengfu's style, elegant and enjoyable, everyone strives to get one … within an hour, calligraphic works in different sizes, scattered everywhere in the cabin.'[36]

THE ELEGANT ART OF RECIPROCITY

A good proportion of a scholar-official's output had its origins in gift-giving practices. That is to say, a large number of works were done for someone, or for a specific occasion. This, in the Ming dynasty scholar-official Wen Zhengming's words, and as discussed in a recent study by Clunas, formed the clearing of an 'elegant (or pure) debt'.[37] Many works in this exhibition can be placed, through their colophons, in this category. In these works, the complex visual and verbal metaphors of abstract art and poetry are given meaning within the rhetoric, as well as within the actual social act of gift-giving.

In addition to existing works which are inscribed for specific friends, a great number of stories, anecdotes, autobiographies and personal letters recorded in the Qing dynasty *biji* (miscellanies notes) help outline the 'obligation' system that governed the circulation of calligraphy during this period, and establish the precise circumstances of the gift occasion and the recipients.

Presenting a peer with a piece of calligraphy was generally done on one's own initiative. It was common practice to present a couplet to people on occasions such as birthdays and weddings or as condolences for a deceased. Calligraphy was also used for farewell messages, encouraging the recipient to reach greater accomplishments. A late Qing mandarin Fang Junshi 方浚師 recalls that in 1868, when he was promoted to a provincial position and about to leave the capital, his mentor and formal boss, the grand secretary Woren 倭仁 (?–1860) presented him with a couplet inciting him to be modest, like the sea embracing hundreds of rivers.[38]

As demonstrated by many works in this exhibition, calligraphy was also done at someone's request. *Suoshu* 索書(requesting a calligraphy) was considered a proper and even 'pure' activity, and the person under request would normally be happy to fulfil such an 'elegant (or pure) debt'. Zhang Zhiwan (cat no 10), who once served as a grand secretary, was described as a very generous mandarin. Even at the age of 80, he would agreeably satisfy whoever came to him requesting a painting or calligraphy on a small fan.[39]

Over his lifetime, a scholar-official might receive countless requests for calligraphy. In clearing such 'elegant debts', different mandarins showed different attitudes or responded differently on different occasions: stingy on some occasions while very generous on others, depending on his mood at the time. Pan Zuyin 潘祖蔭 (1830–90), minister of works during the Tongzhi period, was a connoisseur and collector of antiques. Once he acquired a Han dynasty brush washer from a dealer, who requested Pan write a couplet for him. Upon returning home, Pan immediately wrote the couplet and dispatched a servant to deliver it. After a moment, in great delight, he composed another and again sent it to the dealer.[40]

Some unique or even eccentric reactions towards such a 'request for calligraphy' have been viewed by the Chinese as *yashi* 雅事 or 'elegant behaviour'. Peng Yulin 彭玉麟, minister of the Ministry of War in 1883, for instance, is said to have loved painting and calligraphy, yet never easily did them for others; only if he was willing could he be convinced to produce something, no matter how hard one tried. Once on an official trip he called in at a county, where the magistrate presented him with paper, brush and ink, requesting his calligraphy. On that evening, a chef took the opportunity to serve Peng dinner in order to ask for him for his calligraphy. So Peng agreed, using the materials the magistrate had provided. The next day, he said to the magistrate, 'I have used your paper to write a piece of calligraphy for the chef. Please don't blame me for not fulfilling your request.'[41]

The calligraphy of esteemed scholar-officials was so cherished by their peers that even their perfunctorily written notes would have been collected. Such is the case of Prince Yongxing (cat no 4) and Qian Feng 錢灃 (1740–95), who served as a deputy commissioner of the Office of Transmission and a court censor in Qianlong's reign. According to Ji Chang, the late 19th-century writer, even the receipts written for handing or taking over documents had been taken by their peers or subordinates, and a single character would be treasured as if it were a piece of jade.[42]

Since there were scholar-officials who defied 'social obligation' and seldom gave out their calligraphic works, obtaining examples of their works was a challenge to those fervent lovers of calligraphy. Liu Yong 劉墉 (1719–1804), a grand secretary of Qianlong's court, was rarely willing to brush for others. One of his peers at the Council of State, however, successfully managed to collect a number of his calligraphic works and made them into a thick album to show off: he frequently presented Liu with souvenirs and invited him for dinner, and had hence received numerous handwritten courtesy letters from Liu expressing gratitude![43] In comparison with such acts of what may be described as 'circumventing calligraphy', others resorted to improper means. Liang Tongshu, the esteemed courtier and calligrapher of Qianlong's reign, once travelled to the capital from the south. When passing by Shangdong he paid a visit to the governor, who told him that he could not go further, for a flood had inundated the road. Liang made a temporary stop, waiting for the road to be reopened. He stayed at a hostel provided by the governor where there was not a book to be found, only dozens of ink cakes and hundreds sheets of papers. So all Liang could do to pass the time was calligraphy. Almost a month later, the governor came to inform him that the flood had retreated. Only when Liang resumed his journey did he realise that there had been no flood and that the governor's hospitality was simply a crafty plot to defraud him![44]

A LIFE WITH THE BRUSH

Superb calligraphy requires great skill and years of arduous training. Many scholars in late imperial China devoted, if not all, a great amount of their leisure time to calligraphy. Ji Yun 紀昀 (1724–1805), a *jinshi* of 1754 and chief editor of *Siku quanshu* (*Collectanea of imperial books*), tells us that 'from four to an old age, he had never put aside the brush and the inkstone for a single day'.[45] Chen Kangqi, a scholar-official of the Daoguang and Xianfeng periods (1821–55), who once held the position of the second-class secretary in the Ministry of Punishments, wrote a couplet describing a scholar-official's career as 'Drifting along the sea of officialdom as sea gulls; life and death within books like silverfish'.[46]

The increasing importance of calligraphy created a great demand for calligraphic education from a very young age, and the practice of calligraphy played an important part in the preschool and junior school education, both formal and informal: the formal calligraphic education was provided by one's teacher, parents and school, and the informal from the constant effects of the environment and model examples. There are numerous anecdotes about how children at an age below 10 had dazzled the public with their precocious skill in calligraphy. Zhu Kuntian 朱昆田, son of the famous scholar Zhu Yizun (1629–1709) was said to be capable of practising calligraphy at the age of nine. Prince Yongxing (cat no 4) was also described as a born calligrapher. Wang Shizhen is said to have been able to brush cursive script at the age of nine.

An individual's natural ability, family background, a good teacher, long periods of practice, exposure to a variety of written models, and an ability to innovate upon major styles were the factors thought to contribute most to the maturation of a good calligrapher. Zhu Pengshou, a late Qing scholar-official recalled how his brother stressed the calligraphic education of his son Lianyuan, and had a teacher to guide the little boy's learning. Since Zhu Pengshou was a *jinshi* recipient and an accomplished mandarin, the young calligraphy practitioner would regularly send his homework to him, all the way from Yangzhou in Jiangsu to Beijing, seeking his appraisal. Zhu patiently 'made comments and instructions for each character, discussing in detail the method of structuring; therefore the boy learnt analogy in calligraphy'.[47] After several years the boy passed the child level exam with high honour, and was selected to be enrolled at the state-run county school, preparing for the local level examination. Such is one of the common examples of children who began their *juye* 舉業 (career of civil service examinations).

But this could take many years and become almost an obsession. Sun Qingyuan from Hubei was just such an example. After he passed the provincial level exam, everyday he practised calligraphy by writing an album in large script and another in lesser script; if it was busy during the daytime, he would make up for it in the evening, thus lasting years. The result of the metropolitan exam was that, although he obtained the *jinshi* degree, he did not make it as a Hanlin member. He was so disappointed that he blamed the crisis on his calligraphy and locked himself inside his room to intensify his calligraphy practice. Only when fellow *jinshi* receivers came to comfort him by saying, 'Although we are lucky to make it as members of the Hanlin Academy, your calligraphy is in fact much better than ours!' did his depression subside.[48]

Candidates sometimes practised the script requested for the exam over many years, skilfully refining their script, yet failed at the metropolitan exam. Lu Yitian, a writer of the Jiaqing and Daoguang periods tells us about his fellow townsman Ding Duoying, a contemporary of his uncle, who studied hard and particularly indulged himself by learning *kaishu* (regular script). His practice included doing about 2000 court exam papers, yet all 10 times he tried the exam he failed.[49]

Calligraphy was lifelong learning. Those who succeeded in the examinations and achieved the rewards of holding office did not end their practice there. They would continue to improve their skills in different scripts for various purposes. When Zeng Guofan became a member of the Hanlin Academy, he 'practised *xiaokai* or lesser regular script every day, preparing for the promotion exam (*kaochai* '考差').'[50] His continued learning resulted in the innovation of his calligraphic style: a contemporary commented that his calligraphy showed three major changes – during an early period he followed the script of Liu Gongquan of the Tang; then Huang Tingjian of Northern Song replaced Liu in his middle age; and when he was getting old, Li Yong of Tang and Liu Yong of Qing became the models of his study.[51]

To many scholar-officials, the pursuit of calligraphy spanned a lifetime. Its lifelong practice allowed an individual to write with greater confidence and ease. After his father died, Liang Tongshu retired from the Hanlin Academy to his hometown of Hangzhou, where 'he lived in retirement for 60 years, was a prolific writer with erudition, and excelled in calligraphy. He could produce dozens of calligraphic works every day, and the persons who requested his calligraphy came in droves. Even Japanese and Koreans felt very pleased to get his works'. Recalling a visit from Liang, Qian Yong observed that the retired scholar 'must talk freely about the origin and development of calligraphy to enlighten young men … at the age of 90 he still wrote inscriptions on stele and epitaphs for others; he could work daylong without any weariness'.[52]

Qian Yong also described another scholar-official's calligraphic life, his mentor, Jin An'an 金安安, who had held many government positions, including Guizhou provincial judge, before retiring to his hometown at age 75 to live a simple life. At a young age, his calligraphy followed Yu Shinan of the Tang. As he grew older, he favoured the calligraphy models of the Jin dynasty (265–420). After 40 his enthusiasm shifted from the two Wangs to Zhao Mengfu, and specifically close to Wen Zhengming of the Ming dynasty. Whenever his followers came to ask about calligraphy, he always explained the primary sources of the characters. He could last through the whole day without any fatigue.[53]

THE POETIC MANDARIN

As we learn from the literary accounts, a well-disciplined scholar-official during the Qing period was required to be highly competent and hard-working, but above all to possess admirable skills in calligraphy. He exercised calligraphy with enthusiasm before and after he obtained his position in the civil service; he also had a keen sense of aesthetics, and, seemingly, a constant awareness of his lofty identity as a member of the elite. An elite scholar-official's eccentricity, his romantic sentiment and his dignity as reflected in his love of calligraphy are interestingly embodied in the following anecdote, which relates that in the summer 1865, Feng Zhiyi 馮志沂, a *jinshi* of 1836 and an expert on criminal law, was stuck in Shouzhou (modern-day Anhui) when the city was under siege from the army of the Nian rebellion (an uprising that took place in northern China from 1851 to 1863). He said to the magistrate: 'in the learning about the military, I am a layman. Yet I would follow you to the city wall. You manage and command everything, don't feel trammelled because I am a senior official'. He then mounted the city wall, carrying a large urn with wine, a bottle of ink, and some paper and brushes. He explained his act by saying that 'I am not familiar with military affairs, what can I do daylong sitting on the city wall? It would be better to spend time reading and writing calligraphy. Nevertheless, I will never hesitate to die when the city falls'.[54] Such are the stories that the Chinese took delight in talking about. They have been recounted endlessly by people at different levels, and have become educational models for dignified mandarins.

Calligraphy thus transcended its functional role as a requirement for the civil service exam and a tool of bureaucratic communication, becoming a source of pleasure and spiritual resonance. As Zhang Chao (1650– after 1698), a mandarin who served as a clerk of the Hanlin Academy once declared: 'The ancients said that, if there were no blossoms, moon and beauties, they would not like to be born in this world. I want to add that, if there are no writing brushes, ink, chess and wine, one cannot live as a man'.[55]

1 Fang Bao 方苞 (1668–1749), *Wangxi jiwai wen* 望溪集外文
2 Ma Zonghuo 馬宗霍 (1897–1976), *Shulin jishi* 書林紀事
3 Zheng Jun 震鈞 (1857–1926), *Tianzhi erwen* 天咫偶聞, published in 1907, *juan* 3
4 Wang Shizhen 王士禛 (1634–1711), *Xiangzu biji* 香祖筆記, *juan* 1, 4, 8, *Chibei outan* 池北偶談, *juan* 1, 3, *Fen'gan yuhua* 分甘餘話, *juan* 1, and *Juyilu* 居易錄, *juan shang*
5 Chen Kangqi 陳康祺 (late 19th century), *Langqian jiwen erbi* 郎潛紀聞二筆, *juan* 6
6 Zhu Pengshou 朱彭壽 (act Guangxu period 1875–1908), *Anle kangpingshi suibi* 安樂康平室隨筆, *juan* 1
7 Wang Shizhen, *Xiangzu biji*, *juan* 9
8 Chen Hengqing 陳恒慶 (gained *jinshi* degree in late Qing), *Jianshu xi'an biji* 諫書稀庵筆記
9 He Shengsheng 何聖生, *Yanzui zaji* 簷醉雜記, *juan* 2
10 He Shengsheng, *ibid*; Ge Xucun 葛虛存 (early 20th century), *Qingdai mingren yishi* 清代名人軼事, *xia*,
11 Luo Dunrong 羅惇曧 (1885–?), *Bintui suibi* 賓退隨筆. For Hanlin Academy, see cat no 25.
12 Ge Xucun, *ibid*, *xia*; Sun Jing'an 孫靜庵 (early 20th century), *Qixiage yecheng* 棲霞閣野乘, *juan xia*
13 Niu Xiu 鈕琇 (18th century), *Gusheng xubian* 觚剩續編, *juan* 3
14 Zhaolian 昭槤 (late 18th century), *Xiaoting xulu* 嘯亭續錄, *juan* 5
15 He Shengsheng, *ibid*, *juan* 2
16 Sun Jin'gan, *ibid*, *juan shang*
17 Qian Yong 錢泳, *Lüyuan conghua* 履園叢話, *shang*, *juan* 6
18 Ouyang Zhaoxiong 歐陽兆熊 & Jin Anqing 金安清, *Shuichuang chunyi* 水窗春囈, *juan shang*. See also Kang Youwei 康有爲 (1858–1927), *Guang yizhou shuangji* 廣藝舟雙楫, *juan* 26 'ganlu 幹祿'
19 Liangxi zuoguan laoren 梁溪坐觀老人 (1849–1917), *Qingdai yeji* 清代野記, *juan shang*
20 Chen Kangqi, *Langqian jiwen chubi* 郎潛紀聞初筆, *xia*, *juan* 11
21 Chen Kangqi, *Langqian jiwen erbi*, *juan* 4
22 Ouyang Zhaoxiong & Jin Anqing, *ibid*, *juan shang*
23 Wang Shizhen, *Fen'gan yuhua*, *juan* 2
24 Ma Zonghuo, *Shulin zaojian* 書林藻鑒, *juan* 12
25 Li Jun 李鈞, *Zhuancao riji* 轉漕日記, cited in Ji Chang 繼昌, *Xingsuzhai zaji* 行素齋雜記 (written in 1899), *juan shang*; see also Kuang Zhouyi 況周頤 (1859–1926), *Meilu conghua* 眉廬叢話
26 Ouyang Zhaoxiong & Jin Anqing, *ibid*, *juan shang*
27 Zhu Guozhen 朱國楨, *Yongchuang xiaoping* 湧幢小品, written in 1621, cited in Zhao Jishi 趙吉士 (1628–1706), *Jiyuan suoji* 寄園所寄, *juan* 11
28 Xu Xiling 徐錫齡 and Qian Yong 錢泳, *Xichao xinyu* 熙朝新語, *juan* 8

29 Wu Qingchi 吳慶坻 (late 19th century), *Jiaolang cuolu* 蕉廊脞錄, *juan* 3
30 Sun Dianqi 孫殿起 (1894–1958), *Liulichang shusi siji* 琉璃廠書肆四記
31 Li Dou 李鬥, *Yangzhou huafang lu* 揚州畫舫錄, written in late 18th century, *juan* 2
32 Li Dou, *ibid*, *juan* 2
33 Ouyang Zhaoxiong & Jin Anqing, *ibid*, *juan shang*
34 Qian Yong, *Lüyuan conghua*, *shang*, *juan* 6
35 *Ibid*
36 Ma Jianzhong 馬建忠 (1845–1900), *Dongxing xulu* 東行續錄
37 Craig Clunas, 2004, p 8
38 Fang Junshi 方浚師 (late 19th century), *Jiaoxuan shuilu* 蕉軒隨錄, *xia*, *juan* 10
39 Ji Chang, *ibid*, *juan xia*
40 Chen Hengqing, *ibid*
41 Zhen Jun, *Tianzhi erwen*, *juan* 6
42 Ji Chang, *ibid*, *juan xia*
43 Ge Xucun, *ibid*, *xia*
44 Chen Qiyuan 陳其元 (act mid 19th century), *Yongxianzhai biji* 庸閑齋筆記, *shang*, *juan* 3
45 Chen Kangqi, *Langqian jiwen chubi*, *xia*, *juan* 8
46 Chen Kangqi, *Langqian jiwen chubi*, *xia*, *juan* 8
47 Zhu Pengshou, *ibid*, *juan* 5. See also Kang Youwei, *ibid*, for a general discussion
48 Chen Hengqing, *ibid*
49 Lu Yitian 陸以湉 (early 19th century), *Lenglu zashi* 冷廬雜識, *juan* 2
50 Kuang Zhouyi, *ibid*.; Zeng Guofan, *Zeng Guofan jiashu* 曾國藩家書, 'quanxue pian 勸學篇'
51 Ouyang Zhaoxiong & Jin Anqing, *ibid*, *juan shang*
52 Qian Yong, *Lüyuan conghua*, *shang*, *juan* 6
53 Qian Yong, *ibid*
54 Liangxi zuoguan laoren, *ibid*, *juan xia*
55 Zhang Chao 張潮, *Youmen ying* 幽夢影, written in c1698

士大夫之筆:清代書法藝術的社會史

柳揚

清代重書法,在知識階層,書法甚至高過繪畫。它不僅是視覺藝術,而且是帶有社會政治功能的工具。它與階級地位密切相關。清初的幾位統治者都重視書法,因爲作爲一種精致的文化媒介,書法可以幫助入主中原的滿清穩定其法統地位,並以此贏得漢人士大夫的心。通過不斷賞賜給臣民皇帝親筆書寫的書法,統治者展現了自己無處不在的影響。

對清代書法藝術影響最大的是科舉考試制度,它不光重視候選人的詩文儒學功底,而且還更看重其書法之優劣。這種趨勢在清初就已露出端倪。《郎潛紀聞》説順治乙未會試榜發,世祖將主考者選定的第三名提爲狀元,因爲他認出了該人的書法並且龍顏大悦。有清一代多如牛毛的筆記爲我們描繪出一幅活生生的圖景:書法優者往往在科舉考試中勝出。"説者謂每科新進士三四百人,凡擢大魁者,或擅文名,或工書法,奪標之望,尚不難推測而知。"(朱彭壽)

這樣一來,在朝廷裏擔任文書一類事務的小官吏往往比别人有更多奪魁的機會。比如乾隆庚辰科狀元畢沅、榜眼諸重光,辛巳科探花趙翼,光緒庚辰科狀元黄思永、庚寅科狀元吴魯都是著名的例子。而許多名聲卓著的學者,由於書法欠佳,往往名落孫山,不能入翰林。據説龔自珍因此心懷不滿,令家中所有女子學流行的館閣書。每當客人有言及翰林者,他必嘲笑説:"今日之翰林,猶足道耶?我家婦人,無一不可入翰林者,以其工書法也。"(葛虚存)

除了登科有望,書法精熟者獲得了更多的進入朝廷服務的機會。康熙第五次南巡時曾下詔,令江南上下兩江舉監生員人等,有書法精熟、願赴内廷供奉抄寫者,通過考試擇優錄取。道光時的著名書家錢泳回憶説,當刑部尚書姜晟還在湖南巡撫任上時,偶見其筆墨,遂大稱賞,屢囑部下馳書來聘。由於上下皆重書法,書法成爲科舉和考差聘任的必要條件,一種替人代考的職業應運而生。槍手往往是那些旅京應試工於楷法者,"每逢謄錄供事等試,必爲人代考,或數十金、或百金,視其人之名望分貴賤。"(《清代野記》)

這種看重書法因此可能忽視實際才能的風氣,到了晚清那天崩地裂的當口,其弊端尤其明顯。當時也出現了一些批評的聲音。例如咸豐元年,禦史王茂蔭奏稱:殿試朝考,務重文義,嗣後請讀卷、閱卷大臣不論字體工拙,專取學識過人之卷,進呈欽定,批明刊發,使天下曉然於朝廷所重,在文不在字。咸豐三年金陵落入太平天國軍之手,輿論皆譴責當時的兩江總督陸建瀛誤事。但曾做過刑部員外郎的陳康祺評論説:象這些官吏,本以試帖楷書進身,所以臨危驚慌失措乃是必然的事。(陳康祺《郎潛紀聞二筆》)

由於統治者對書法的重視,時尚的書風逐時而變,皆窺上意所在。康熙年間,由於聖祖喜董其昌書法,一時文臣皆從之。雍正、乾隆年間則流行以顏眞卿字爲根底而間以趙孟頫和米芾書風。嘉慶一變而爲歐體。道光再變而爲柳體,時稱翰林院爲柳衙,南書房爲深柳讀書堂。科舉考試中對書法的強調以及官僚書風的發展,形成了一種富有時代特色的所謂"館閣體"。館閣體乃是在楷書的基礎上吸收歐、趙兩種風格演變而成,但是卻完全消除了歐、趙的個性,變得比楷書還要中規中矩。有清一代館閣體成爲科舉考試與官方文書中所使用的正統書體。人們無不以它爲學書的根基。

在清代,書法首先是功能性的,它是一個官吏在日常事務中必備的工具。首先,手書上疏的質量,往往能影響其官宦生涯。明代曾任吏部尚書的朱國楨在《湧幢小品》中提及,兵部尚書胡宗憲被彈劾,但嘉靖皇帝同情他,因爲他不獨有禦寇之功,且先後上疏,皆手書如一,説明他對皇上有敬謹心。這種上疏必手書的傳統在清代依然重視。張大有爲漕運總督時,奏言寫字手顫,請奏摺代書。上諭云:"忙時令人代書亦可,若密摺仍須親寫。即字畫粗大,略帶行草,亦屬無妨。辭達而已,敬不在此。"《熙朝新語》的作者評論説,我朝待大臣之寬容脱略如此。這説明在其它時候,要求會嚴格得多。

由於科舉制度看重書法,清代士大夫大多是書法高手,他們的書法因此爲社會所重。祠堂會館的題字,墓誌碑文的撰寫,乃至店鋪之名等等,往往出自他們之手。除此之外,他們還在風景名勝,佛寺道觀,留下大量詩文墨跡。

同僚或上下級之間的書法往來,構成了清代書法藝術的另一個現象。索書被視爲雅事。而不同的人,或相同的人在不同的環境對待被索書的態度,則往往不同。有的大方,如曾任大學士的張之萬,年屆八旬,有索書畫者,輒欣然應之。有的則不輕易爲人作書,如劉墉。所以,想方設法得到著名同僚書家的作品,便成了愛好書法的官吏們的一個心事。有的靠智取:如劉墉的一個同僚常送他禮物請他吃飯,因此得到不少劉的感謝函。有的則取下策來騙取:有一個山東的地方官騙路過的梁同書説前面路被洪水所阻,因此留其住了月餘。客房中除紙筆墨外別無它物。所以這位曾任翰林學士的書法家只有靠寫字打發時間,這些作品自然都落入房主人的囊中。

書法是同僚之間交流的最佳方式,它也可以幫助官吏與其轄地的百姓溝通。《揚州畫舫錄》説揚州太守高承爵善書,爲民愛慕,每歲暮,鄉民求書福字以爲瑞。書法還是不同文化間交流的橋梁。1682年汪楫出使琉球,應邀爲其國王寫擘窠大書,王驚以爲神。1882年出使朝鮮的馬建忠回憶説,返航之前,兩國官員在船上互贈書法以作別。

在清代,書法成爲每一個有上進心的人的必修功課,而且是終生的學業。紀昀説自己"自四歲至老,未嘗一日離筆硯。"它是科舉考試的敲門磚,而進入仕途之後,還要不停地練習完善,以應付各種考差以及社會性的需要。曾國藩在其家書中説自己在官翰林時,亦日書小楷,以備考差。而對很多人來説,書法也是一種審美的需求,一種人生的態度。同治乙丑夏,進士馮志沂在壽州爲捻軍所困,他對刺史説:我於軍事是外行,你且全權指揮,不要因爲我是上官而束手束腳。他於是攜一巨甕酒,墨汁一盂,紙筆若干,書若干而登城。他解釋説:"既爲守土官,城亡與亡耳。我不嫻軍旅事,終日據城樓何所事,不如仍以讀書作字消遣也。"如同這樣的"美談"所揭示的,書法因此超越了各種各樣功利性的作用,成爲精神的需求。正如17世紀曾任職翰林的張潮所説:"昔人云:若無花、月、美人,不願生此世界。予益一語云:若無翰、墨、棋、酒,不必定作人身。"[節譯]

COLLECTING CHINESE CALLIGRAPHY: A PERSONAL JOURNEY

James Hayes

Neither art historian nor artist, why and how did I come to collect the calligraphy of Chinese scholar-officials of the Qing period? The answer lies in my working life in Hong Kong, and my passion for history.

It began with going to Hong Kong in 1956 as (you might say) a British colonial mandarin in the making.[1] First, I was required to learn some Chinese at the Language School of the University (there was only one in those days) and a year later I was sent to work in the then rural New Territories. This was, and is, the 945 square kilometres of mountain, plain and islands added in 1898 by long lease to the older, ceded, Colony of Hong Kong, whose life as a British possession had begun during the Opium War of 1839–42.

For a supposedly small place like Hong Kong, the New Territories turned out to be quite large. My own district – yes, there was a District Administration with four district officers under a district commissioner – took in a wide swathe of sea, islands and mainland across the southern half of the New Territories. It contained about 70 000 people living in 180 villages and several large market townships which were also anchorages for many boat people and their fishing craft. The mainland New Territories took in the remaining 520 villages, more market towns and the large multi-village settlements of the major lineages of the territory, known collectively as the Five Great Clans.

Then there were the people, and the plentiful traces of their past, for the New Territories had been continuously settled since the 12th century, and perhaps even before. Laying down local history had always been an honoured tradition in China, and New Territories' folk had lived up to their obligations. There were enough surviving commemorative tablets from old temples, ancestral halls, schools, bridges and the like to fill three volumes of historical inscriptions, published by the former Hong Kong Urban Council in 1986, while others have been recorded since.

These historical tablets of dark grey slate-like stone (the surfaces could flake off with time and exposure to the elements) were quite distinctive, and usually contained hundreds of closely cut characters. They provided the names of the managers responsible for organising construction or repairs, together with those of all the donors, however small their contributions. I am emphasising these memorials because history was my basic motivation when I began to collect.

Old buildings provided another rich source of historical artefacts. The villages of the Five Great Clans contained ancestral halls and other large structures constructed in the solid and picturesque style of the regional architecture, with plentiful decoration in wood, stone and stucco, inside and out. Their names (and those of the calligraphers) were borne on large painted boards, or carved into granite lintels above the entrances. They had first been written on paper and then transferred by artisans into stone or wood. The interiors contained other signed items in the same style, including 'honour boards' recording imperial examination titles won by members of the local lineages or by kinfolk living elsewhere. However, the skilled artisans who did this work, and also cut the commemorative tablets, seem always to be anonymous, seldom if ever honoured. Nor were their techniques described by the scholars who wrote about Chinese calligraphy.

Calligraphy was everywhere in Old China – for that was what the rural New Territories still was in the 1950s. Besides the large ancestral halls, calligraphy featured in the external and interior decor and fittings of many better-class houses – not forgetting the auspicious couplets on paper, renewed in each succeeding lunar new year at every door of every home, no matter how humble. Buddhist and Taoist monasteries and nunneries also contained calligraphy and paintings, as did the larger restaurants in the city. So, too, did the home of one of my respected friends, a well-to-do elderly merchant and shopkeeper of Tai O on Lantau Island, who was the head of the township's committee of elders.

The antithetical couplet – written vertically on each side of two hanging scrolls, beginning with the right – had become popular among scholars in the late Ming dynasty. It was an elegant literary form, with prescribed rules that taxed the writer's poetic skills, and his mastery of words and allusions. By the 18th century (mid Qing) the couplet was universally favoured for recording friendship or esteem, commemorating birthdays, eulogising the departed and marking many different occasions. Couplets can comprise varying numbers of characters, but the larger sets, requiring longer lengths, can only be hung in places with high walls, such as in reception rooms and ancestral halls.

The calligraphers whose names were to be found on couplets or perpetuated in wood and stone were, I discovered, usually men with imperial degrees, and often scholar-officials. If you were a successful scholar, it was natural to want to be an official too, for in Old China they were at the top of the social ladder. It is interesting to see that officials headed the lists on commemorative tablets, although their donations were much smaller than the principal subscribers, who were usually prosperous shopkeepers and local gentry.

At that time, I was learning rather than collecting. And indeed there was so much to learn.

I began to look out for any surviving scholars – not very likely, since the last imperial examinations had been held in 1905, but there were still a few around. There was even one scholar-official, a Cantonese who had held medium level posts in central China before the 1911 revolution which ended the Manchu dynasty.

From these gentlemen I gleaned much about the educational system which led to success in the examinations for the fortunate few. Not the first foreigner to be vastly impressed, I was awed by the huge feats of memory that were almost commonplace through the practice of learning whole texts off by heart, as was required of candidates. It was aptly said by a successful participant, 'Officials were honoured, because learning itself was honoured in China'. And learning and examinations in those days meant the Confucian and other classical books.

I was a natural Confucian. Always fond of Alexander Pope's works, I discovered that his famous *Essay on man* ('Know then thyself, presume not God to scan / The proper study of Mankind is Man') had echoed the Sage, of whom he wrote: 'Superior and alone Confucius stood / Who taught that useful science – to be good'. Since Confucianism was the bedrock of the Qing state and the creed of its officials and gentry, you might say that I was already half-way to collecting their calligraphy. But that came later.

My initial collecting had been documentary. My first published article (1962), on the New Territories in 1898, had owed much to inscriptions and documents from the villages. I had also begun to look around the back streets of the city, where I discovered the stalls and modest shops of dealers in anything old, from furniture to art objects. Owing to the demolition of many old shop-houses and homes for redevelopment, much came their way, including old land deeds and family papers on a variety of subjects. At the urgings of a friend, Dr Ramon H Myers, scholar-curator of the East Asian Collection at the Hoover Institution in Stanford, California, I began also to purchase documents on its behalf, and continued to do so for many years.

In the shops and stalls where I looked for anything interesting, old paintings by Cantonese artists were occasionally on sale. Ignoring the more favoured (and more expensive) ones of the Lingnan school of the early 20th century, I began to collect the more traditional 19th-century productions. After finding that calligraphies were also to be had, and rather short-sightedly tiring of the paintings, I sold them back to the dealers. Thus I began to collect calligraphies in their original form – written on paper or silk – as opposed to simply admiring those transposed onto wood or stone.

At that time (in the 1970s) they were not expensive. Like the porcelain and pottery of the province, works by most Cantonese artists and calligraphers were not very highly regarded by the art world (although local art museums already had small collections). And in the places that I frequented, they cost less than in art dealers' galleries, which of course suited my pocket. At this point, I must introduce you to my friends, the stall holders and minor dealers of the day, giving their names in romanised Cantonese.

There was 'Robber' Lee, as I and some friends called him affectionately, because his asking prices were usually on the steep side. He had a tiny off-street room on Hollywood Road on Hong Kong Island, and he and his son were my cheerful friends and providers of books, scrolls, paintings, porcelain and much else, in indifferent condition but usually interesting, for over 35 years. He loved Chinese opera and was forever singing to himself when not chatting with his Western and Chinese customers or browbeating one of the first-line 'collectors' from old houses and shops who was trying to sell him his latest load. His English was fractured and inventive. He used to write short descriptions of his goods, and these were sometimes side-bursting, as when a demure and well-dressed young Cantonese lady of early Republican times, whose photograph was for sale, was billed as 'a famouse [sic] hooker'.

Then there was Mr Chan, who occupied the rear section of a small stationery shop kept by a pleasant woman with a family of young children. He sold art objects and books, and brought many calligraphies my way. But his business zeal was affected by his passion for the turf on race days. He and his friends would crowd the shop, and as also happened when mah-jong games were in full swing, little business could be done. His friends all knew me. Upon noticing my approach, one called out 'Ah Chan, your godfather has arrived', from which I deduced that I was seen as (to put the best face on it) a sure thing! But Mr Chan got one of his headmaster friends, Mr Wong Man-cheuk, to write a couplet for me, which they presented before we left Hong Kong for Australia, a touching memento of our friendship.

Mr Ho, Mr Sze and another Mr Chan (Peter) in Cat Street, the curio area below the Man Mo temple in another part of Hollywood Road, were other old and valued acquaintances from whom I bought regularly over the years, as was Mr Sit of the Sam Yick Bookshop in Wanchai, where another art dealer, Richard Yip, more up-market this time, had many calligraphies for sale in the 1970s and early 1980s.

I greatly valued their cheerful friendship and what they did to advance my collecting. They were always willing to let me take items home, and I could buy or not buy as I saw fit, leaving price to be settled on my return visit. Because they stayed open late, I could call in on my daily drive home from the New Territories. These short visits eased the tiredness and stresses of the day's work, for we were all kept very busy in those years of Hong Kong's redevelopment.

Like most collectors, I had to rely on my wits in deciding what to buy. Luckily, I developed a rudimentary test for old pieces. This was to hold an item against the light, whereby any damage was more apparent, and to see whether it had already been repaired or remounted. Also, artists' names could be checked in various publications. Authenticity and personal history were the things that mattered, condition less; albeit art-loving insects, the alternate damp and dry climate of Hong Kong and the Canton Delta, and descendants' or later owners' occasional neglect and indifference, had taken their toll. However, remounting was not as expensive then as it is today, and I was fortunate to have another old friend of long standing, Mr Cheung of Dor Po Chai in Wanchai, who (like his father, since deceased) is a master of this wonderful, almost magical transformation process.

There were other quandaries. At some stage in my collecting, I was told that it was not 'done', during or after remounting, to ink over any white areas left on the brushstrokes (characters) from previous insect activity. Thereby, I missed out on a number of otherwise interesting pieces. The one I most remember (and most keenly regret) was a couplet in 'seal' characters by Chen Li (1810–82), his preferred and best-known script. I was also ever wary of 'big' names. I once found a damaged album scroll purportedly by Liu Yong (1720–1805), Hanlin of 1752, a grand secretary, and a nationally renowned calligrapher. I did not buy, but made a copy. To this day, I am not sure if the scroll was genuine. Perhaps it was! Like fishermen, all collectors have stories of 'the big one that got away'!

Why were these calligraphies so readily available in Hong Kong at the time? Several factors were involved. First, in polite Cantonese society in the late 19th century, it was usual for scholar-officials to present their calligraphies to friends and colleagues, and for persons in their wider circle to request them to do so. My late mother-in-law, born near Canton in 1907, told me that many scrolls and couplets had been kept in her father's home – he was a degree holder – and in her husband's merchant family also. Their association with local gentry and officials in the literary and artistic clubs so popular in that period was doubtless responsible for this. Secondly, the Cantonese merchants of 19th-century Hong Kong lived in two worlds. Establishing themselves firmly there, they took good care to maintain links with their home areas, making charitable donations and remaining part of local society. Also, it was then common for wealthy merchants to purchase degrees and rank, so as to have access to officials and be able to mix socially with them. Probably for all these reasons, over many years of collecting from small dealers, much of whose stock came from street collectors of old things, I found that the homes of many of Hong Kong's moderately well-to-do shopkeepers had been repositories of a wide range of cultural objects, including the calligraphies.

Thus many of my purchases were likely to be of local origin, and not imported from Canton and elsewhere, as was the case following the start of China's modernisation from around 1980. Of course, I cannot be so certain about the sources of the major dealers' stocks, though at that period of my collecting these were still unlikely to be speculative imports owing to Cantonese art objects not being much in vogue. I was certainly fortunate to collect in this field at so favourable a time.

My major collecting ended in 1990, when we came to live in Australia. I had down-sized my collections, including calligraphy, before we left. Many of my scholar-official scrolls and couplets went to the Hoover Institution, by sale and donation. But the lure of these special items still bit deep. I slowly built up another collection, not quite so numerous, and not solely Guangdong like the first, but including scholar-officials from other provinces. These are the items donated to the Art Gallery of New South Wales, on show in the exhibition to which this catalogue provides a guide. To round off this account of my collecting, a list of the items in the Hoover Institution is also included in this publication.

In conclusion, this very special genre, derived from systems of education and government which lasted for almost two millennia, peaked in the period covered by the collection. It had been enriched by the investigative scholarship of mid Qing, which through archaeology and epigraphy made the ancient scripts from the Late Bronze Age and the Han more accessible to the gifted calligraphers, who were also senior officials of the final century of imperial rule.

They, and it, have left a memorable legacy, recognised by all those in a position to know. One such was my professor at the Hong Kong University Language School, the late F S Drake. Born of missionary parents in Qufu, Shandong, in 1892, and a noted Chinese scholar, in an obituary notice for a distinguished contemporary, like himself China-born, Drake wrote feelingly of 'the spaciousness of the closing years of Imperial China … an experience that leaves its mark upon all who have had it'. This was the environment in which our scholar-officials flourished, taking us to the very roots of their achievements.

1 My official rank was that of cadet officer, class two, on a three-year probation, during which I had to pass language and law examinations. In Chinese the term used meant 'student official'

我的中國書法收藏

許舒

我的中國書法收藏始於1956年，當我作爲一個英國殖民地見習官員到香港任職。我先在大學裏學了一些中文，然後被派到新界工作。

在新界，很多地方都能見到寫滿字的石碑：在寺廟，祖祠，學校，石橋。通常上面刻了上百的字，記錄修建組織者以及捐助者的名字。此外，那裏的老建築是提供歷史藝術品的另一個來源。在祖祠中我們可以看見族人中舉的‘進士牌’。的確，五十年代的新界，書法隨處可見：祖祠裏外以及富裕人家，佛道寺廟，以及城市裏的餐館。至於對聯則更是遍佈於於家家户户。

我發現，那些保存下來的書法的作者往往是獲得進士的文人官吏。在紀念碑上，那些官員儘管所捐不多，但往往排在眾人的前面。出於好奇，我開始尋找碩果僅存的中過舉的文人。從他們我瞭解到許多有關科舉考試的知識。我爲他們那熟誦儒家經典的記憶力而傾倒。我自己本人也是個天生的儒家信奉者。這樣，這些學者官吏的書法對我更富有了吸引力。

我最早的收集是與文獻有關的。我發表的第一篇關於新界的文章就得益於我從村子裏收集到的各種銘文和文獻。我開始去一些背街的小店鋪轉悠，那裏可以買到形形色色的舊東西。正好當時我一個在美國斯坦福大學胡佛研究所負責東亞收藏品的朋友請我替他們收購一些文獻性的文物，這樣，我就開始了收藏。

當時，在古董店裏像嶺南畫派之類的作品也時有所見。但是它們價格比較貴，買的人也比較多。於是我轉而收藏更傳統的19世紀的作品，尤其是書法。這些作品在70年代的時候還不是很貴，因爲當時廣東畫家書法家的作品還不怎麼被看重。而且，我常去的那些地方，古物的價格比起古董商畫廊中的東西要便宜得多。

我和那些店鋪的主人成了很好的朋友。他們總是讓我把東西先拿回去，然後再決定要還是不要。因爲他們的店鋪通常開得很晚，所以我往往在下班回返家的途中去拜訪他們。這些短暫的停留使我忘記了一天工作的疲勞。

我的主要收藏活動終於1990，當我移居澳洲之際。在我離開香港之前，我已經開始縮小我的藏品。有一部分或買或送（全出自廣東書法家之手），進了胡佛研究所。但是慢慢地我又聚積了另一批書法作品，它們出自清代來自各地的士大夫書家之手。它們就是這一批我捐給新南威爾士藝術博物館的東西，大部份呈現在這個展覽中。[節譯]

Zheng Xiaoxu, *Two poems in running script* (detail, cat no 28)

要吳論書家欲下石如拜
豈可耐石庵號蘊藉堆墨
州所陣不挂鎧何筆曉若
林喻飛鳥我意在無礙題
腕若背相語絕頂初晴看

CATALOGUE

1 FENG Chengxiu 馮成修 (1702–1796)

Couplet in running script 行書五言聯

pair of hanging scrolls; ink on paper, 32.5 x 154.5 cm each 275.2003.a-b

露濃花氣重，風細竹聲幽。
款識：展程仁兄先生。潛齋馮成修。
鈐印：潛齋。馮成修印。南史之章。

The scent of flowers becomes more intense as the dew gets heavier;
The sound of bamboo is serene when the wind blows gently.

Inscription and signature: For Mr Zhancheng. Feng Chengxiu, style name Qianzhai.

The poem in this couplet is taken from various sources. The first line was modified from a verse by Zhang Xiaoxiang of the Northern Song dynasty.[1] The scent of flowers and the elegant bamboo hint at a serene and secluded garden retreat, surroundings that are conducive to study and meditation.

Feng Chengxiu (alias Dafu 達夫, style name Qianzhai 潛齋) is a good example of the successful scholar-official rising from humble beginnings. He was born in Nanhai, Guangdong, and after his father disappeared while he was very young, Feng drifted about, destitute, finally settling in neighbouring Yangxi county. Legend has it that Feng once had a dream in which he was accompanied by a servant holding a banner bearing his official title 'Guizhou xuezheng 學正' (director of education). This dream encouraged Feng to apply himself to his studies.[2] In 1739 at the age of 37, he gained his *jinshi* degree (the degree for the highest civil service examination). He was made a bachelor of the prestigious Hanlin Academy, and thereafter was appointed to various government positions, including senior secretary of the Ministry of Rites.[3]

The calligraphic style Feng demonstrates in this work, so-called *xingshu* or running script, lies somewhere between the regular (*kaishu*) and cursive (*caoshu*) scripts, in that at times the strokes are controlled and regular, and at other times free-flowing and informal. In general it is a simplification of the early regular forms, developed into stabilised and independent script types after the Han dynasty. From the late 17th to early 18th centuries, the stylish and graceful calligraphy (mainly running script) of Dong Qichang (1555–1636) was very popular because of Emperor Kangxi's preference for it. However, during Qianlong's reign (1736–95), imperial taste shifted to the brisk, well-knit style of Zhao Mengfu (1254–1322). Although quite different in style, elegance and grace characterised the calligraphy of both Dong and Zhao, and this is demonstrated in this couplet.

1 Zhang Xiaoxiang (1132–69), 'In a flowering season, the heaven resembles river 菩薩蠻・花月天如水'

2 Li Boyuan 李伯元, *Nanting sihua* 南亭四話 [Shanghai: Shanghai shudian, 1985], *juan* 6, p 395

3 For life of Feng Chengxiu, see *Qing shigao* (History of the Qing dynasty), [Zhonghua Press, Beijing, 1977], *Biography* 257

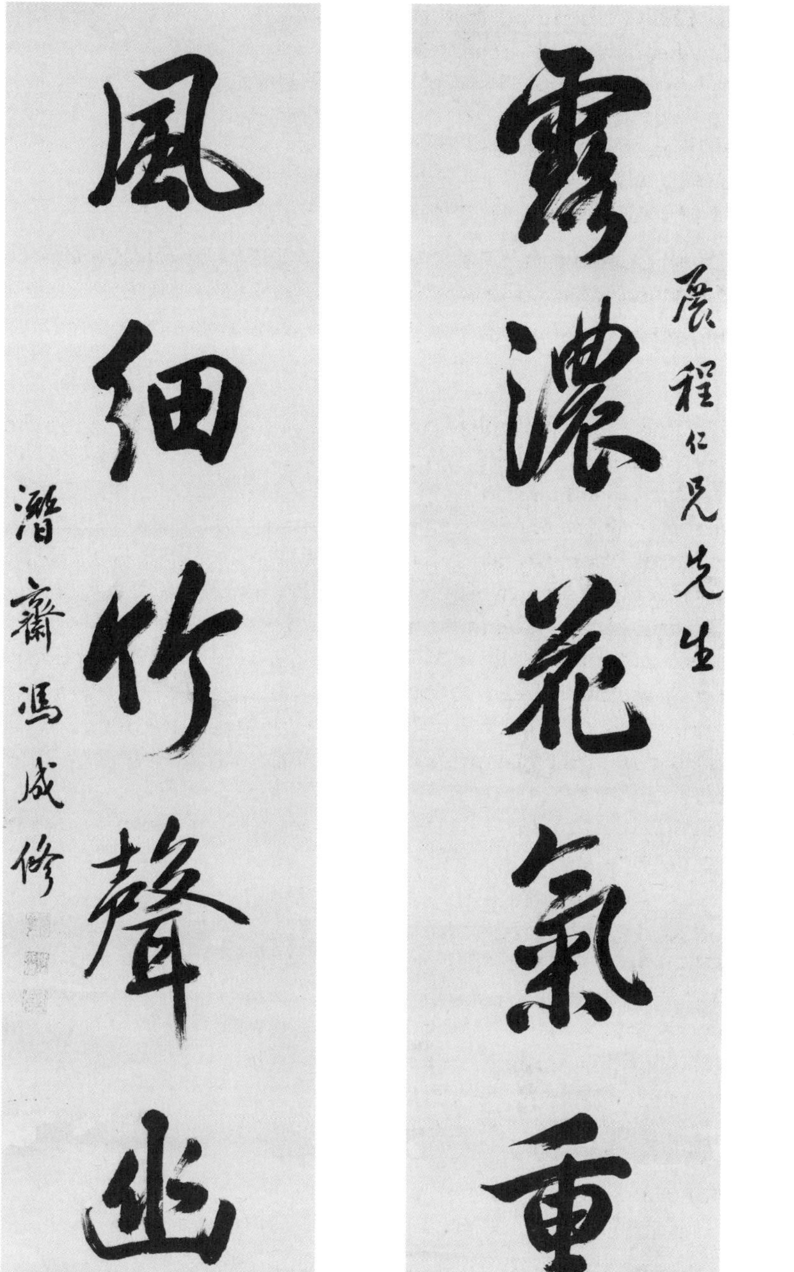
露濃花氣重
風細竹聲幽
潛齋馮成修

2 CAO Xiuxian 曹秀先 (1708–1784)

Couplet in running script 行書集杜審言詩五言聯

pair of hanging scrolls; ink on paper, 35.2 x 147.5 each 302.2003.a-b

學摠八千卷，文傾三百篇。
款識：地山秀先。
鈐印：秀山之印。

[Your] *knowledge embraces eight thousand volumes of books;*
[Your] *literary grace goes beyond that shown in the 'Three hundred poems'.*

Inscription and signature: Xiuxian, style name Dishan.

This couplet is borrowed from a poem by Du Shenyan of the Tang dynasty[1] which was written in praise of a courier named Li Sizhen, who was dispatched as an envoy to Hedong (in modern Shanxi). The 'Three hundred poems' in the second line normally refers to *Shijing* (Book of odes), an anthology of poems dating from the late 12th to 6th centuries BCE. In general the lines are a compliment to a scholar for his outstanding knowledge and elegant writing style.

Cao Xiuxian (alias Hengsuo 恆所, style name Dishan 地山) was a native of Xinjian in Jiangxi province. In 1736 he gained the rare opportunity of taking a special imperial *jinshi* examination that was set for candidates with extraordinary talents, and he excelled in it. As a successful courtier, he held senior positions in various ministries, including the Ministry of Rites and the Council of State. Because of his profound knowledge and high moral character he was appointed Grand Tutor to the Heir Apparent. He was also one of the chief editors of the multi-volumed *Siku quanshu* or *Collectanea of imperial books*, compiled under imperial auspices in 1787. After his death, Emperor Jiaqing (r1796–1820) conferred the posthumous title of *wenke* 文恪 (cultivated and scrupulous) on Cao, in recognition of his literary accomplishments and firm loyalty to the government.[2]

Cao was an eminent calligrapher of the time; Qianlong once called him *dashoubi* 大手筆 ('a compelling brush'). Both Dong Qichang and Zhao Mengfu's styles are natural and unrestrained, elegant and refined. However, for some scholars they lacked strength and vigour. Thus it became the fashion during the reigns of emperors Yongzheng (r 1723–1735) and Qianlong to use the Tang dynasty calligrapher Yan Zhenqing's calligraphy as the preferred model. Over this foundation, the elegant styles of Dong and Zhao were then adopted. Cao's work shows the influence of Yan, in its grandeur and loftiness, as well as the gracefulness of Dong's and Zhao's styles.

1 Du Shenyan (c 645–708), 'Written for Li Sizhen while he was dispatched as an envoy to Hedong 和李大夫嗣眞奉使存撫河東'

2 For life of Cao Xiuxian, see *Qing shigao, Biography* 321

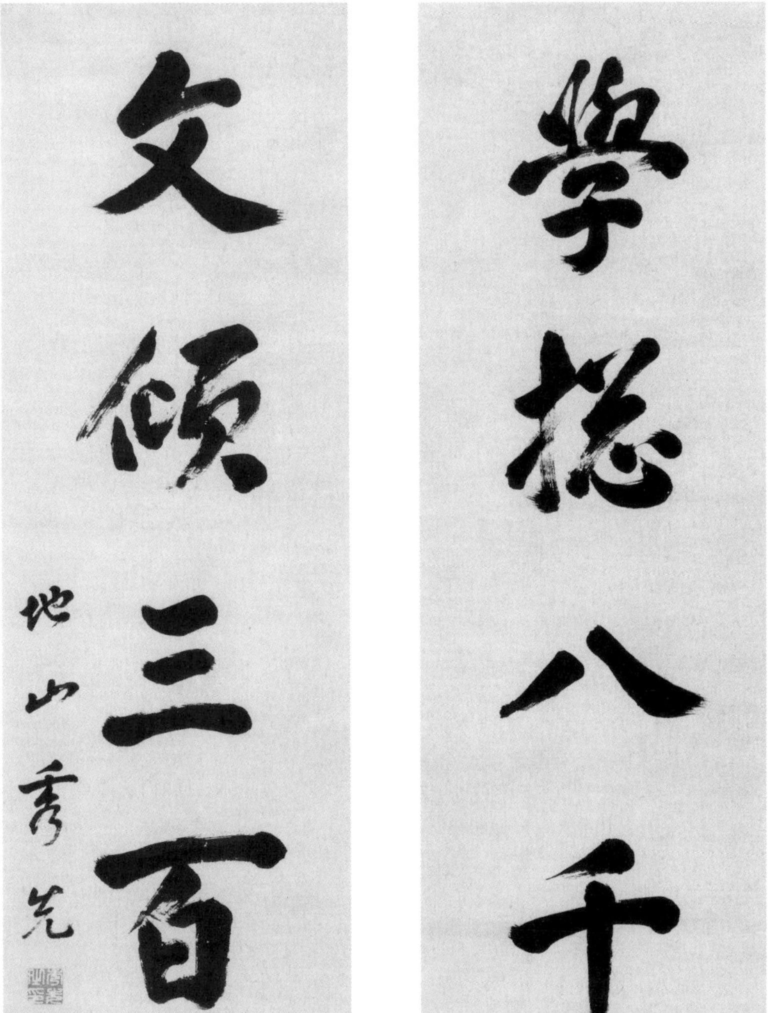
學總八千卷
文傾三百篇
地山秀光

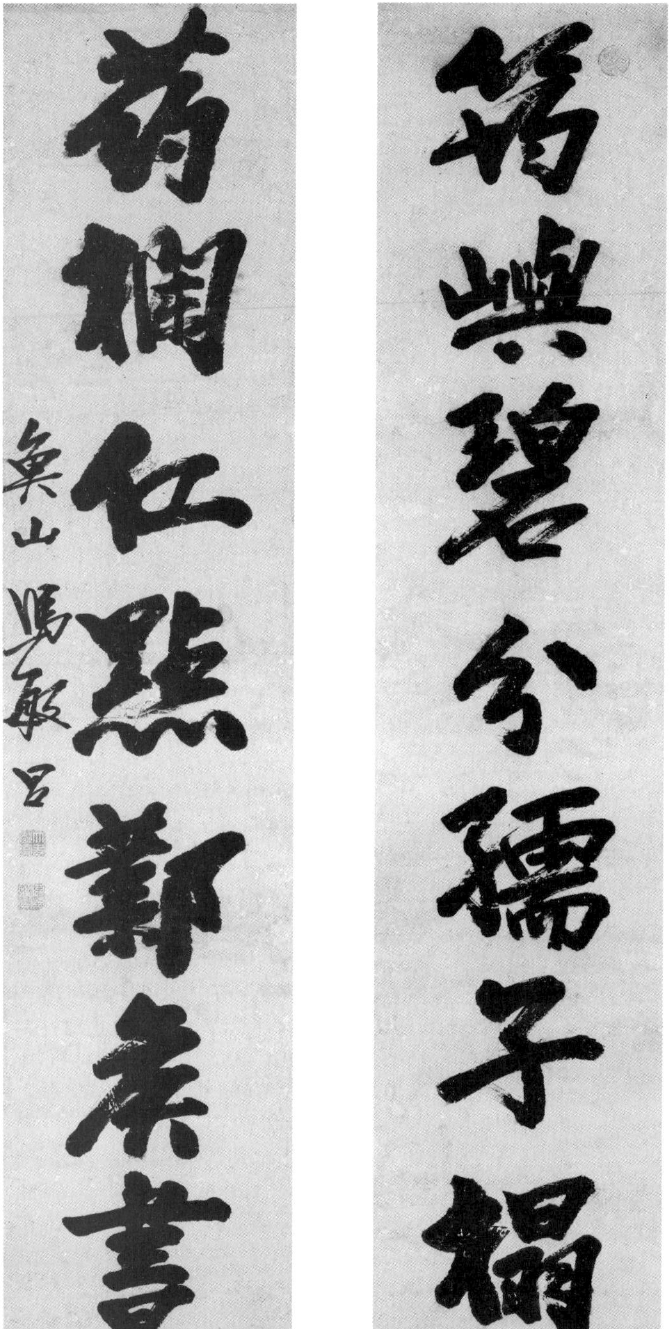

3 FENG Minchang 馮敏昌 (1747–1807)

Couplet in running script 行書七言聯

pair of hanging scrolls; ink on paper, 40 x 198.5 cm each 276.2003.a-b

筠嶼碧分孺子榻；葯欄紅點鄴侯書。
款識：魚山馮敏昌。
鈐印：長毋相忘。太史都官。馮敏昌印。

The green of the bamboo hillocks enhances the couch of Ruzi;
The red of the peony garden sets off Yuhou's study.

Inscription and signature: Feng Minchang, style name Yushan.

This couplet would have been a gift to a scholar friend. Intended as a compliment, it alludes to two distinguished historical figures, thus likening the recipient to them. The first line hints at a story recorded in the Han dynasty official history *Houhanshu*, which tells how when Chen Fan was governor of Yuzhang (in present Jiangxi) he only entertained one guest, Xu Ruzi, a retired scholar with a high moral reputation. Chen made a couch specially for Xu, which was suspended from the ceiling after Xu left, so no one else could use it. The second line alludes to the Tang dynasty prime minister Li Bi (722–789). The emperor conferred on Li the title of Yehou (Duke of Ye). Disgusted by the political struggles at court, he withdrew to the southern sacred mountain Hengshan and lived there for almost ten years, keeping over 10 000 books in his study.

Feng (alias Boqiu 伯求, style name Yushan 魚山) was a native of Qinzhou in Guangdong. A *jinshi* of 1778, he was a *bianxiu* (compiler) at the imperial Hanlin Academy. He held several senior official positions such as deputy secretary of the Ministry of Revenue, and retired to Guangdong, where he became a renowned educator. Feng was both a prolific writer and a distinguished calligrapher.[1] From Qianlong's reign onward an ongoing interest in learning calligraphy from earlier models emerged as an alternative to the Wang Xizhi tradition. Many scholars preferred the more vigorous models of the ancient inscriptions recovered from bronzes and stone monuments, particularly the calligraphy engraved on stele from the Northern dynasty (439–581). This trend is called *beixue* (school of stele study). Feng is considered one of the pioneers of this school, particularly in his native province of Guangdong. As well as being an advocate of the Northern stele calligraphy style, Feng also favoured the calligraphy of Huang Tingjian (1045–1105) of the Northern Song dynasty, whose influence is seen in this work, particularly in the thickness and strength of the stroke, which is dramatised by the great range of ink tones. The work shows a vigorous strength different from the graceful style current at the time in the mandarin circle.

1 See *Qing shigao*, *Biography*, 272

4 **YONGXING** 永瑆 (1752–1823)

Couplet in running-regular script 行楷集韓愈、庾信詩七言聯

pair of hanging scrolls; ink on paper, 161.2 x 33.3 cm each

鸞翔鳳翥眾仙下，珠聯璧合重光來。
款識：篔坡先生清賞，成親王。
鈐印：成親王。

While the mythical birds 'laun' hover and phoenixes soar aloft, celestial beings descend;
Perfectly matched pearls on a string, and pieces of jade forming a beautiful whole, together shed a double light.

Inscription and signature: For the pure appreciation of Mr Yunpo, [composed by] Prince Cheng.

Couplets in China served various purposes. It was common practice to present a couplet on occasions such as birthdays and weddings, or as condolences after a death. Wedding couplets always included the customary auspicious images. In this example, the first line was taken from a poem composed by the renowned Tang dynasty poet Han Yu. The second line was from a poem by the Northern Zhou poet Yu Xin.[1] Perfectly matched pearls are on a string; jade rings are mutually enhanced by association with each other; these images, together with auspicious birds and celestial beings, create a suitable metaphor for an excellent match.

Yongxing (alias Jingquan 鏡泉, style name Shaoan 少厰), better known as Cheng Qingwang or Prince Cheng, was the eleventh son of the emperor Qianlong. From a young age, he excelled in calligraphy, even arousing the admiration of the emperor himself. During his father's reign, he was appointed one of the chiefs in charge of editing the *Collectanea of imperial books*. He led an enjoyable artistic life dedicated to the study of calligraphy and poetry, except for a year or so, during his brother Jiaqing's reign in 1799, when he temporarily undertook two positions as acting minister for the Board of Revenue and as minister of the Board of Civil Office.[2] His noble status allowed him a life of luxury and learning, and allowed him access to many ancient masterpieces in the imperial collection. In his early years of calligraphic training Yongxing followed the style of Ouyang Xun (557–641) of the Tang and later Zhao Mengfu, as was the fashion, especially within the royal family circle. The result was a calligraphic style known as 'foundation of Ou, surface of Zhao', meaning a combination of the two styles, vigorous yet elegant. As reflected in many of Yongxing's extant works, Zhao Mengfu played a key role in the formation of his mature style. The couplet is written in an informal regular script: it contains elements of running script.

1 Han Yu (768–824), 'Song of stone drum 石鼓歌'; Yu Xin (513–581), 'Song of heavenly altar 周祀圜丘歌：昭夏'
2 For a brief introduction of Yongxing's life, see *Qing shigao, Biography*, 8

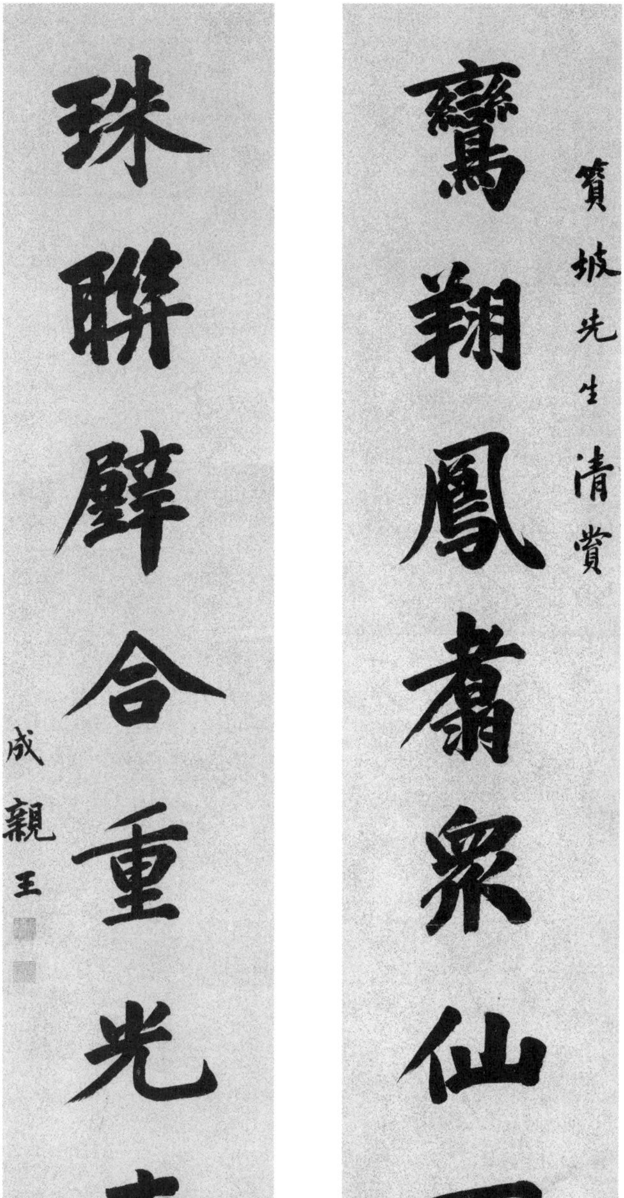
寶坡先生清賞
鸞翔鳳翥衆仙下
珠聯璧合重光来
成親王

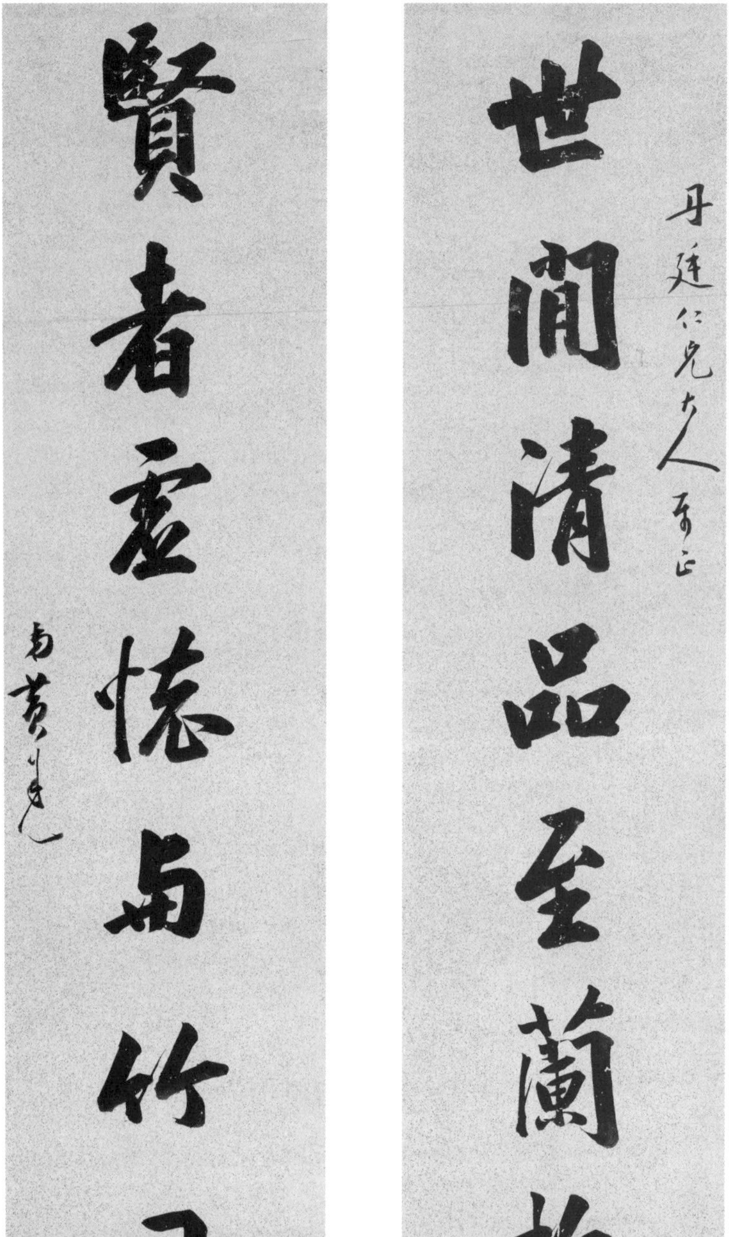
世間清品至蘭極
賢者虛懷與竹同

5 **HUANG Danshu** 黄丹書 (1757–1808)

Couplet in running script 行書七言聯

pair of hanging scrolls; ink on paper, 126.8 x 30. 2 cm each

世間清品至蘭極；賢者虛懷與竹同。
款識：丹廷仁兄大人雅正。弟黄丹書。

In a mundane world, with the orchid the pure spirit reaches the extreme;
And the modest mind of a worthy person resembles the bamboo.

Inscription and signature: For the appraisal of Mr Danting; written by Huang Danshu.

In traditional Chinese culture, numerous features of nature symbolised human moral qualities. The orchid was prized primarily for its delicacy. Its fragrance was thought to be ethereal, yet so pervasive as to 'steal into one's sleeves' almost unnoticed, thus symbolising the exemplary character of the superior gentleman. Bamboo has a hollow interior, which suggests an unassuming, open mind. Apparently this couplet was a gift extolling the high moral character of the recipient.

It is uncertain whether or not Huang himself composed the couplet. It was included in *Remarks on selected couplets* 楹聯叢話, compiled in 1840 by Liang Zhangju 梁章鉅 (1775–1849), and in *An assembly of calligraphy and couplets by the Zhizu Studio* 知足齋集禊序楹帖 by Zheng Kaixi 鄭開禧 (who gained the *jinshi* in 1814).

Huang Danshu (alias Tingshou 廷授, style name Xuzhou 虛舟) was a native of Shunde, Guangdong province. He gained the provincial *juren* degree in 1795, but failed in the metropolitan *jinshi* examination. He was appointed an educational administrative position at Kaiping County in Guangdong and later became the administrator of the famous Yuxiu Academy in Guangzhou. Huang was admired in that region for his *sanjue* (the Three Perfections), in poetry, calligraphy and painting. Having published three anthologies of poetry, he was honoured, along with three other scholars, as one of the Four Masters of the Lingnan (Guangdong) region.

Huang is best known for his *caoshu* (cursive style) and *lishu* (clerical style) calligraphy. Yet what is demonstrated in this couplet is running script, which is written elegantly, reflecting early Qing taste which favoured the running and cursive scripts of the past masters. During the Jiaqing reign (r1796–1820), a new trend in calligraphy emerged, in which the seal and clerical scripts were emphasised because of the enthusiasm in ancient stele inscriptions, yet the preference for running and cursive scripts persisted. Ever since emperors Kangxi and Qianlong had declared the styles of Dong Qichang and Zhao Mengfu to be the orthodox paradigm, the tradition of *tiexue* (the study of classical calligraphy models) was enhanced by imperially commissioned compendiums of model calligraphies, engraved on stone and widely distributed as prints. It is no surprise then, that mandarins all excelled in running script.

6 LIANG Airu 梁藹如 (1769–1840)

Couplet in seal script 篆書五言聯

pair of hanging scrolls; ink on paper, 36.8 x 200 cm each 294.2003.a-b

探道三茅洞，遊仙五老峰。
款識：青崖。
鈐印：梁藹如印。青崖。

Exploring the Way at the Three Mao Grottoes;
Cultivating immortality on the Peaks of Five Saints.

Signature: Qingya

'Three Mao Grottoes' refer to Mount Mao located southwest of present-day Zhenjiang in Jiangsu province. The name was taken from the three Mao brothers, who in the mid 2nd century BCE made the three main peaks their home and became immortal. Daoists have crowned Mount Mao as one of the greatest sacred mountains in China. The 'Peaks of Five Saints' refer to either the mountain region located in Lushan in Jiangxi province or one other in Yongji, Shanxi province – both traditionally regarded as Daoist sacred mountains.

Liang Airu (alias Yuanwen 遠文, style name Qingya 青崖) was a native of Shunde in Guangdong. He obtained the *jinshi* degree in 1814, and was appointed secretary of the Grand Secretariat. He made a comprehensive study of the earlier styles of calligraphy and soon excelled in different types of scripts. He was also a well-known poet and painter.

The couplet is written in what is known as *zhuanshu* (seal script), which developed during the Qin dynasty (221–207 BCE) as a standard for the new empire, and was ascribed to Li Si (d208 BCE), the chief minister of the time. One of Li's inscriptions has been preserved. The so-called Yishanbei 嶧山碑 stele was inscribed during the Qin first emperor's inspection tours in 219 BCE. The original stele was destroyed before the early 8th century, but was re-erected with inscriptions re-engraved in 993, and is now in Xi'an. It was the script on this stele (so-called *xiaozhuan* or 'lesser seal' script) that Liang Airu followed. A typical feature of this script is the uniformity of size and shape of the characters. The brush strokes are round and have a supple quality. The evenness demonstrates painstaking execution. In comparison with the seal script of the Qin period, Liang's strokes are fuller.

During the late Qianlong and Jiaqing periods, there was some anxiety that the current style had been overshadowed by the suave elegance of Dong Qichang and Zhao Mengfu, and some scholars turned to the script and style popular from monuments of the Qin to Northern dynasties. They wanted to reinvigorate calligraphy with a creative revival of antique styles. Liang Airu's couplet was composed against such a background.

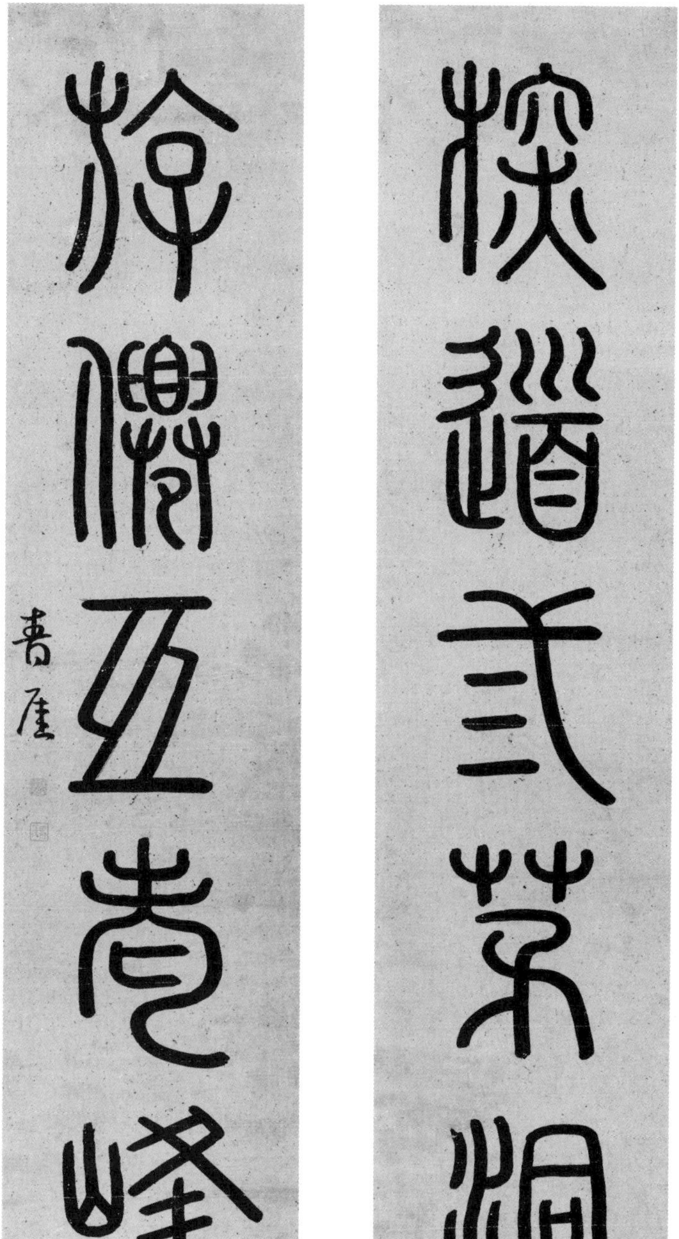

7 CHEN Qikun 陳其錕 (*jinshi* 1826)

'Zhang Xu's comment on calligraphy' in cursive script 草書張旭書論

hanging scroll; ink on paper, 180.6 x 38.5 cm 279.2003

其次在於佈置，不慢不越，巧使合宜；其次紙筆精佳；其次變法[化]適懷，縱舍掣奪，鹹有規矩。五者備矣，然後能齊於古人。
款識：其錕
鈐印：陳其錕印。棠谿。

[In regards to calligraphy] *Next is disposition: it should not be too relaxed, yet not overstep the bounds, making it ingeniously appropriate. Then there is the quality paper and brush. Then the proper alterations – no matter if releasing or seizing* [the brushes], *both should suit the established practice. If* [one's calligraphy] *possesses all these five qualities, it then can be equal to the ancients.*

Inscription and signature: Qikun.

Chen Qikun (alias Wushan吾山, style name Tangxi棠谿) was a well-known calligrapher of the Guangdong region during the Daoguang period (r1821–50). A native of Panyu (in present-day Guangzhou), he gained his *jinshi* degree in 1826, and was assistant secretary for the Ministry of Ceremonies. Later in life, he lectured at the Yangcheng Academy in Guangzhou for some 30 years. He was a connoisseur and master of the *qin*, a seven-stringed instrument similar to the zither.

Chen's composition in this hanging scroll is a segment taken from a longer discussion on calligraphy by the Tang dynasty calligrapher Zhang Xu (early 8th century). When Zhang was asked by his student, the then young Yan Zhenqing, about how one's calligraphy could become as good as the ancients, Zhang put forward five principles: brush handling; awareness of brush method; disposition; superb paper and brush; and appropriate alteration of the rule. He advised that if one's calligraphy had all five qualities, then one could match the ancients for excellence. This hanging scroll contains only three of these five principles, and is possibly the last piece of a set of two.

The script Chen used in this work is appropriate for the content. *Caoshu* (cursive script) evolved in the Eastern Han (25–220 CE) and reached its peak in the Tang dynasty. The characters vary in size in the same piece of writing. They are generally executed swiftly, with the strokes running together or joining up, and with the last stroke of the first character merging into the initial stroke of the next, producing a kind of visual continuity from top to bottom. The irregular lines and the fluid relationships between the words allowed the calligrapher considerable compositional freedom. Zhang Xu was a great master at *caoshu*, noted for the complete abandon with which he applied the brush. It is said that he would not set about writing until he had become drunk.

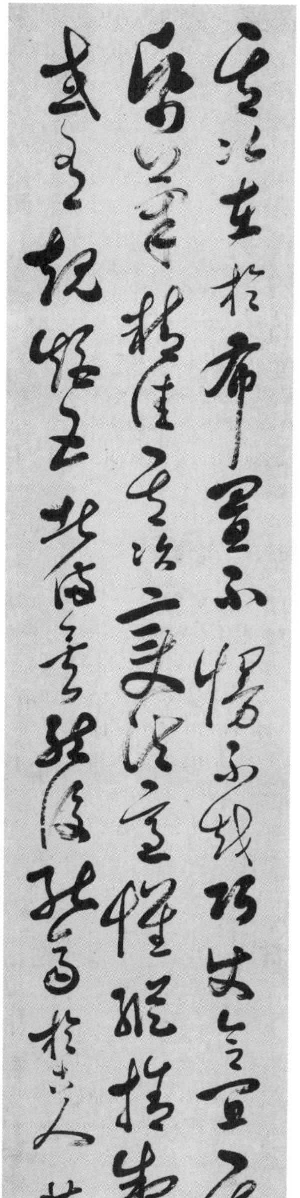

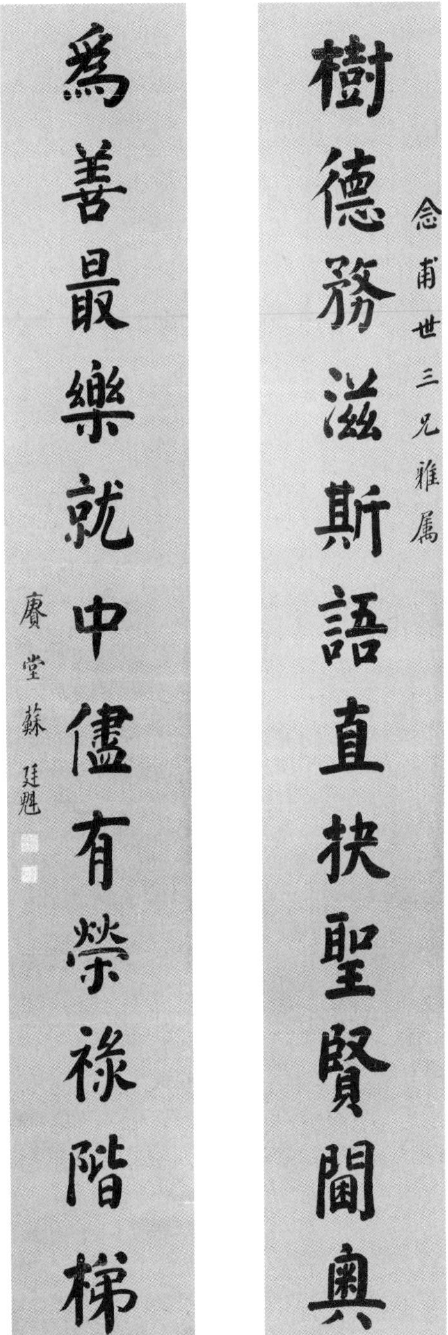
樹德務滋斯語直抉聖賢閫奧
念甫世三兄雅屬
為善最樂就中儘有榮祿階梯
賡堂蘇廷魁

8 **SU Tingkui** 蘇廷魁 (1800–1878)

Couplet in regular script 楷書十二言聯

pair of hanging scrolls; ink on paper, 44.2 x 270.5 cm each 282.2003.a-b

樹德務滋，斯語直抉聖賢閫奥；爲善最樂，就中盡有榮華富祿階梯。
款識：念甫世三兄雅屬。賡堂蘇廷魁。
鈐印：蘇廷魁印。賡堂。

If planting virtue, make sure your plants will grow and spread;
This saying describes the most profound essence of a sage.
To be at one's happiest one should perform benevolent deeds;
This saying is a stepping-stone to fortune and glory.

Inscription and signature: Written for Nianfu as he requested, Su Tingkui, style name Gengtang.

The idiom in the first line was taken from *Shangshu* or *Book of documents* (one of the Thirteen Classics), a text compiled in the late Shang and early Zhou dynasties.[1] The second line alludes to a story from the Eastern Han dynasty: when Prince Liu Cang was asked what would make him happiest, he replied, 'performing benevolent deeds'.[2] The couplet would be considered a suitable motto for scholar-officials conducting their government service.

Su Tingkui (alias Gengtang 賡堂) was a native of Gaoyao in Guangdong. In 1835, he was granted the title of *jinshi*, becoming a compiler at the Hanlin Academy. Soon after he was appointed *yushi* (censor). His upright nature and outspoken style were hailed not only by his colleagues, but even by the emperor. In 1858, when the British and French allies attacked Guangdong, he played a key role in organising the local militia forces to resist the invaders. In the early 1860s, he was appointed treasurer of Henan, then governor-general of Donghe, undertaking dredging the Yellow River to prevent flooding.[3]

The couplet is written in *kaishu* (regular script). This script developed at the end of the Han dynasty, but reached its zenith in the 7th century. One of the most famous calligraphers of this style at the time was Yan Zhenqing, whose style was imitated by many who came after him. Yan's style in this script reflects strength, boldness and grandness. Su Tingkui's script in the couplet is very close to Yan's style, emphasising both composure and firmness in the brushstroke, tenderly managing brush lines within powerful frames. Yan's style was popular with scholar-officials, not just for aesthetic reasons, but also because of its consistency, as the Chinese believe that the style of one's calligraphy truly reflects one's inner nature.

1 *Shangshu*, in chapter of 'Taishi 泰誓'
2 Fan Ye, *Hou hanshu* [Beijing: Zhonghua Press, 1965], 'Biography of Liu Cang'
3 See *Qing shigao, Biography* 165

9 CHEN Li 陳澧 (1810–1882)

Couplet in seal script 篆書集《稧帖》八言聯

pair of hanging scrolls; ink on paper, 167 x 29 cm each 283.2003.a-b

言與蘭清，氣同竹長；情猶水靜，品若山崇。
款識：集稧帖字。陳澧蘭甫。
鈐印：陳澧之印。蘭甫。

The words are as pure as orchids, the breath is as long as bamboo;
The sentiment is as quiet as water, and the moral character is as lofty as mountains.

Inscription and signature: Words adopted from *Lanting xu*, Chen Li, alias Lanfu.

In traditional Chinese culture, the natural attributes of the orchid, bamboo, water and mountain symbolised the moral qualities of human beings. The orchid is an emblem of the triumphant purity of noble men; bamboo is a robust evergreen capable of withstanding the winter snow; it has *jie* 節 (nodes), which is a homophone of *qijie* 氣節 (moral integrity) – it bends but never breaks. In Confucian teaching, water and mountain were metaphors for virtue, or for a higher state of mind. This is reflected in one of the most well-known Confucian dictums, 'The wise man finds joy on the water, the benevolent man finds joy in the mountains'. The analogy between water and mind is commonly found in Chinese writings – Zhu Xi (1130–1200), the neo-Confucian philosopher of the 12th century once said, 'If the mind can be compared to water, then one's disposition is just like calm water, affection resembles flowing water, and desire is similar to waves of water'.[1] Nevertheless, Chen Li's couplet, in part, may not be considered as simply copying Zhu Xi's words. As he mentions in the inscription, he was putting together characters or phrases taken from the famous calligraphic piece, the *Lanting xu* (Preface to the poems composed during a spring party at the Orchid Pavilion) by Wang Xizhi (written in 353). *Jizi* (putting together words) or *jiju* (putting together sentences) from a famous calligraphic piece was a popular practice when composing a couplet, enhancing its literary allusion and creating an aura by linking it to masterpieces of the past.

Chen Li (alias Lanfu 蘭甫, style name Dongshu 東塾) was a native of modern Guangzhou, who composed poetry from the age of nine. At the age of 17, he gained his *xiucai* degree at the prefectural level of the imperial civil service examination; at 27, he obtained the *juren* degree. However, between l833 and 1852 he made seven, unsuccessful, attempts at passing the *jinshi* degree. He only took up minor positions such as *xundao,* or sub-director of studies, in Heyuan county in Guangdong, and director of the Xuehaitang Academy in Guangzhou. Failure to achieve his ambitions in officialdom turned him to scholarly research, and he later became a great scholar in a wide range of fields such as astronomy, geography, history, mathematics, poetry, phonology and linguistics, and wrote numerous books.

Chen Li was particularly renowned for his seal script. During his time, the models of seal script to be followed by practitioners were broadened, embracing a wide range of ancient styles such as those found on inscriptions rediscovered from stele, seals and bronzes. Unlike Liang Airu, who followed the Qin seal script, Chen Li chose the 'Stone Drum' inscription of Zhou Dynasty (c8th BCE) as his calligraphic model. These 'drums' are ten granite blocks in the shape of drums unearthed in the 7th century, each engraved with an inscription about rulers' hunting activities. During the late Qing dynasty these inscriptions were regarded as an orthodox model for seal script study. In comparison with Liang Airu's couplet, the brush line of Chen Li's seal script appears relaxed, lacking constraint and rigidity.

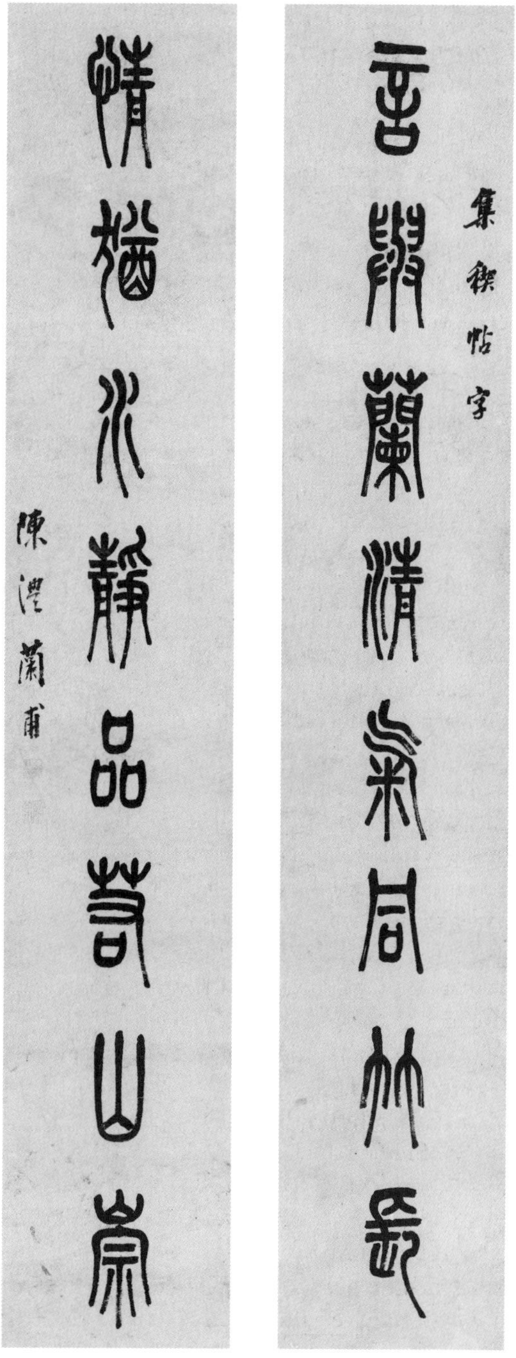

1 Zhu Xi, *Zhizi yulei* 朱子語類, *juan* 5

10 ZHANG Zhiwan 張之萬 (1811–1897)

Couplet in running script 行書七言聯

pair of hanging scrolls; ink on paper, 36.1 x 168 each 288.2003.a-b

風因得竹若殊遇；水不在山無激流。
款識：崑泉三弟雅屬，子青。萬。
鈐印：之萬。子青。

It's a real treat when the wind encounters bamboos;
There will be no rapids if the stream does not flow on a mountain.

Inscription and signature: Written for Mr Hunquan as he requested. [Zhi]wang, alias Ziqing.

When the wind blows through a bamboo grove, it manifests itself in a distortion of the bamboo's shape, while the latter also reveals its momentum by receiving a blow from the wind. The allusion is about the mutual support that increases efficiency: each in a pair shines more brilliantly in the other's company. The second line implies that an adverse circumstance will arouse one's strength.

Zhang Zhiwan (alias Ziqing 子青) was from Nanpi, Hebei province. He passed his provincial *juren* examination in 1840 and in 1847 he received the *jinshi* degree with highest honours (*zhangyuan*), thus being seen in a favourable light by the court. He was a successful official who became grand secretary, and was appointed a tutor in the Imperial Study. Other posts included vice-minister of the Ministry of Rites, governor of Henan and Jiangsu provinces and minister of the ministries of War and Justice. He was later awarded the title of the Grand Guardian of the Heir Apparent. In general, he was considered a conservative bureaucrat, not like his younger brother Zhang Zhidong who explored Western methods in the context of remedying the dynastic decline.[1]

Like many other scholar-officials, Zhang excelled in poetry, and was also well known for his landscape painting, which followed the 16th-century Wu school. Although he lived during the reigns of Daoguang (r1821–50) and Xianfeng (r1851–60) when *beixue* (stele study) was in vogue, Zhang's style as reflected in this couplet shows a *tiexue* tradition, and the strong influnce of Dong Qichang.

1 For Zhang Zhiwan's life, see *Qing shigao, Biography* 225; Arthur Hummel, 1943, pp 32–34

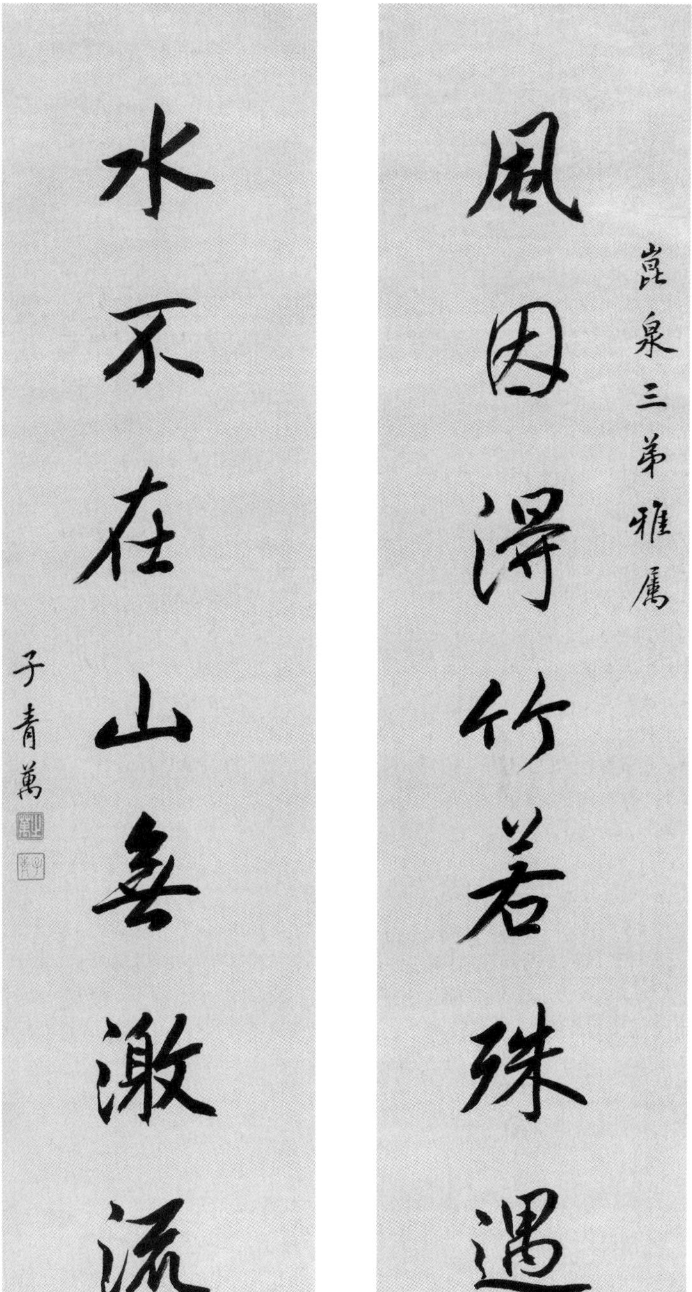
崑泉三弟雅屬
風因得竹若殊遇
水不在山無激流
子青萬

11 ZUO Zongtang 左宗棠 (1812–1885)

Couplet in running script 行書七言聯

pair of hanging scrolls, ink on paper, 141 cm x 34.8 cm each 254.2003.a-b

仁慈性是長生海；靈妙心如九曲珠。
款識：子成四兄屬。左宗棠。
鈐印：大學士章。青宮太保恪靖侯。

A merciful nature is the source of longevity;
The wise mind resembles the complexity of a pearl shell's twists.

Inscription and signature: Written for Zicheng as he requested. Zuo Zongtang.

A native of Xiangyin, Hunan province, Zuo Zongtang (alias 季高, style name Pucun 樸存) was an eminent figure of 19th-century China. His fame as a military leader and statesman almost overwhelmed his achievements in calligraphy. He studied geography and military strategy in his youth, and received the *juren* degree in 1832. Recognition of his talent by Zeng Guofan (elder brother of Zeng Guoquan), one of the most important military leaders in modern history, and Emperor Xianfeng (r 1851–1861), initiated his long military career. As the left hand of Zeng, he served the Qing regime for some 30 years, suppressing various rebellions including the Taiping uprising.[1]

In spite of his arduous duties, Zuo Zongtang was a renowned calligrapher, even during his own times. Although his best-known calligraphy is *xiaozhuan* (lesser seal script), a style developed during the Qin dynasty (221–206 BCE), his skill in *xingshu* (running script), is excellent too, as demonstrated in this couplet. The derivation of his style from *xiaozhuan* is observable. As one can see, here the smooth and regular manner of the seal script has been merged into the elegance of the running script style.

Although the couplet is undated, on the basis of a seal on the work it is tenable that it was done during the last decade of his life. The characters contained in this seal, 'Qinggong taibao' refer to an honourable title, Grand Guardian of the Heir Apparent, that was bestowed on him by the imperial house after Zuo Zongtang recaptured the city Hangzhou from the Taiping rebels in 1864.

1 See *Qing shigao, Biography* 412; Hummel, pp 762–67

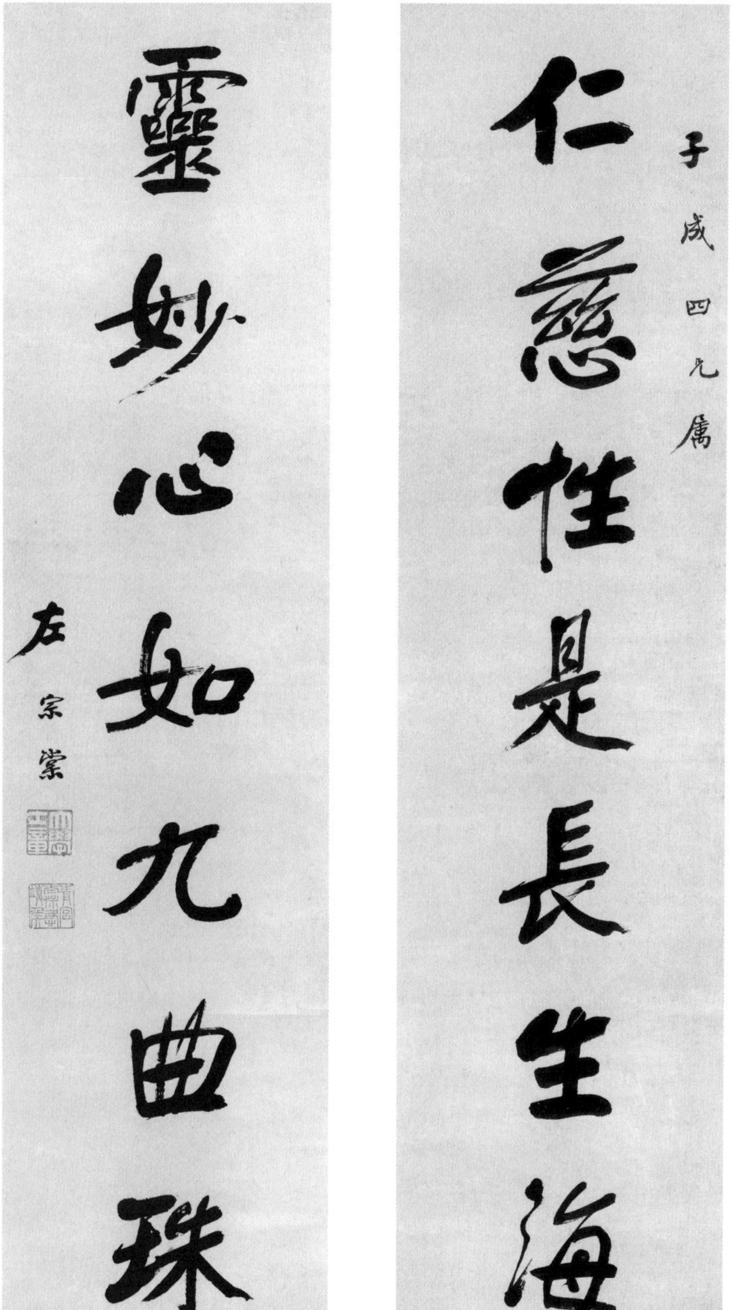
仁慈性是長生海
靈妙心如九曲珠
左宗棠

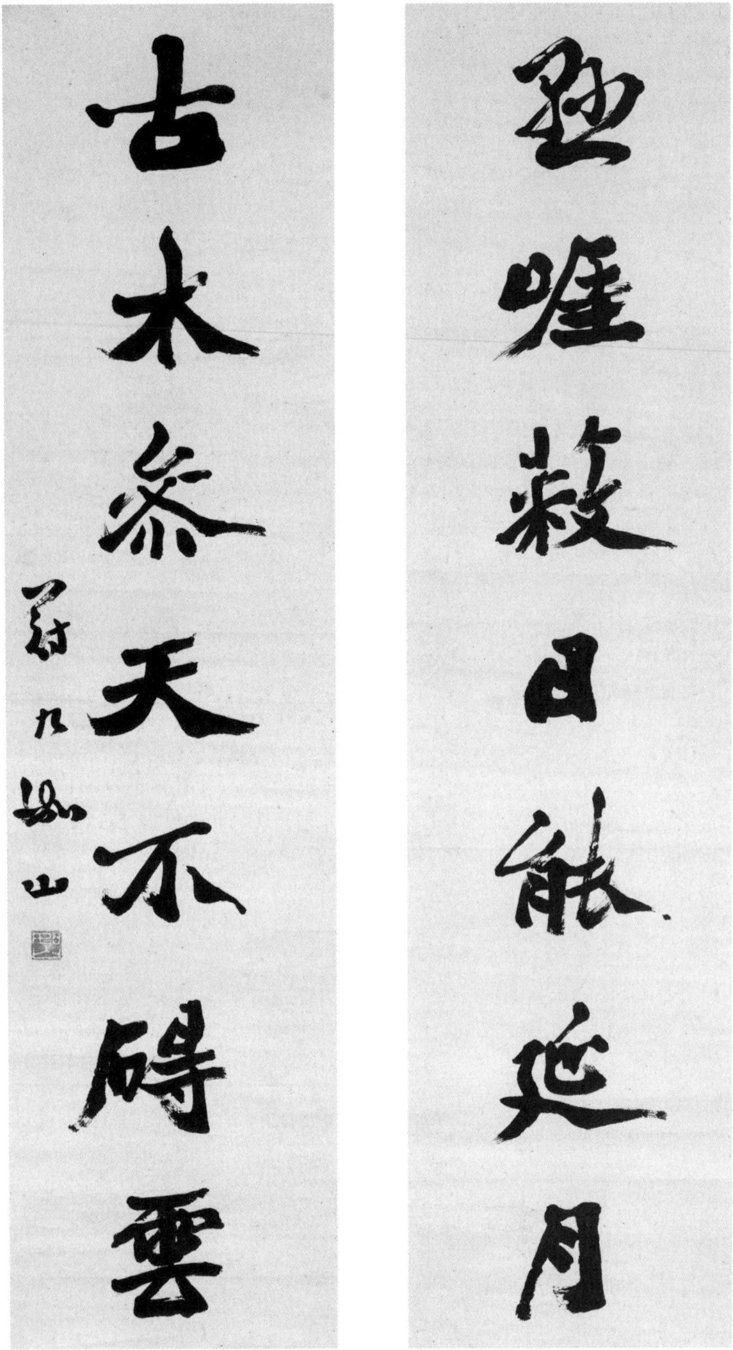
古木參天不礙雲

12 **RUSHAN** 如山 (1815 – after 1885)

Couplet in running script 行書七言聯

pair of hanging scrolls; ink on paper, 125 x 30.7 cm

懸崖敝日能延月，古木參天不礙雲。
款識：冠九如山。
鈐印：如山。

Precipices block the sun, yet lure the moon;
The aged tree reaching for the sky never obscures the clouds.

Inscription and signature: Rushan, alias Guanjiu.

Rushan (alias Guanjiu 冠九, style name Guxi nanzi 古稀男子) was born into a Manchu family. He passed the civil service examination to gain the *jinshi* degree in 1838. He then had a series of official posts, serving as chief comptroller of Jiangsu provincial revenue, as Zhejiang provincial judge, and then as governor of Sichuan. He was well versed in literature and wrote beautiful poetry. Buddhism also exercised a great influence on him.[1]

Rushan admired the style of inscriptions of the Northern Wei stele, and took this as the foundation for his own calligraphy. On this basis, he absorbed and synthesised styles of different scripts, forming his own distinguished calligraphy. This couplet is written in running script, revealing a strong influence from the writings of the Northern Wei stele. Rushan occasionally painted landscapes, using his fingers instead of a brush. His contemporaries compared him with another technically innovative painter, Gao Qipei (1660–1734), who also used his hands – palms, fingers and nails – in place of the traditional Chinese brush.

1 See Du Wenlan (1851–81), *Qiyuan cihua* 憩園詞話, *juan* 5

13 **CHEN Pu** 陳璞 (1820–1887)

Couplet in running script 行書七言聯

pair of hanging scrolls; ink on paper, 40.8 x 175 cm each 281.2003.a-b

早春重引江湖興；嬾性從來水竹居。
款識：君綬姻世清屬。陳璞
鈐印：陳璞私印。古樵。

The early spring again stirs one's distant thoughts;
With unperturbed nature the bamboo always prefers to dwell next to the water.

Inscription and signature: Composed at the request of Junshou, a relative by marriage. Chen Pu.

In Chinese literature *jianghu* 江湖 (rivers and lakes) is a metaphor for the phenomenal world. To escape from *jianghu* is to eschew official careers, fame and other social burdens and to live in seclusion, whereas to be concerned with *jianghu* is to make a commitment to be part of society and to pursue an official career. Withdrawal from society or engagement with it – 'to be or not to be' – was a dilemma the Chinese intellectual often faced: on the one hand, the Confucian ideal demanded one seek an official career under a sage ruler; on the other hand, Daoism encouraged one to pursue the simplicity of a peaceful and unfettered life, in which one may indulge in scholarship or art. This predicament is expressed in this couplet. It conjures up the contradictory sentiment in the mind of the writer: a hesitation at the crossroads of withdrawal from, or participation, in government service. The couplet itself comes from two separate poems by the great Tang poet Du Fu (712–70 CE).[1] The antithetical balance in meaning between the two lines gives the couplet a sense of contemplation.

Chen Pu (alias Ziyu 子瑜, style name Guqiao 古樵, or Chigang guiqiao 尺岡歸樵), was a native of Panyu, in present-day Guangzhou. He gained the *juren* degree at the provincial level examinations in 1844 (some sources say 1851). He served as magistrate of Anfu county in Jiangxi, but soon returned to Guangdong, dedicating himself to education and art; for decades he was the director of the Xuehaitang Academy in Guangzhou.

Chen Pu excelled at regular and running script, but specialised in the latter. He was a fervent follower of the *tiexue* (study of classical calligraphy models). His early calligraphy studies were based on the style of Mi Fu (1051–1107) from the Song dynasty and Dong Qichang from the Ming dynasty. He considered himself a proponent of the classical semi-cursive style of Wang Xizhi (act 320–60), which was the foundation of the *tiexue* movement.

1 Du Fu, 'Two poems written at "Man's day" 人日兩篇', and 'A poem written in response to Mr Yan's 'Pavilion in open country' 奉酬嚴公寄題野亭之作'.

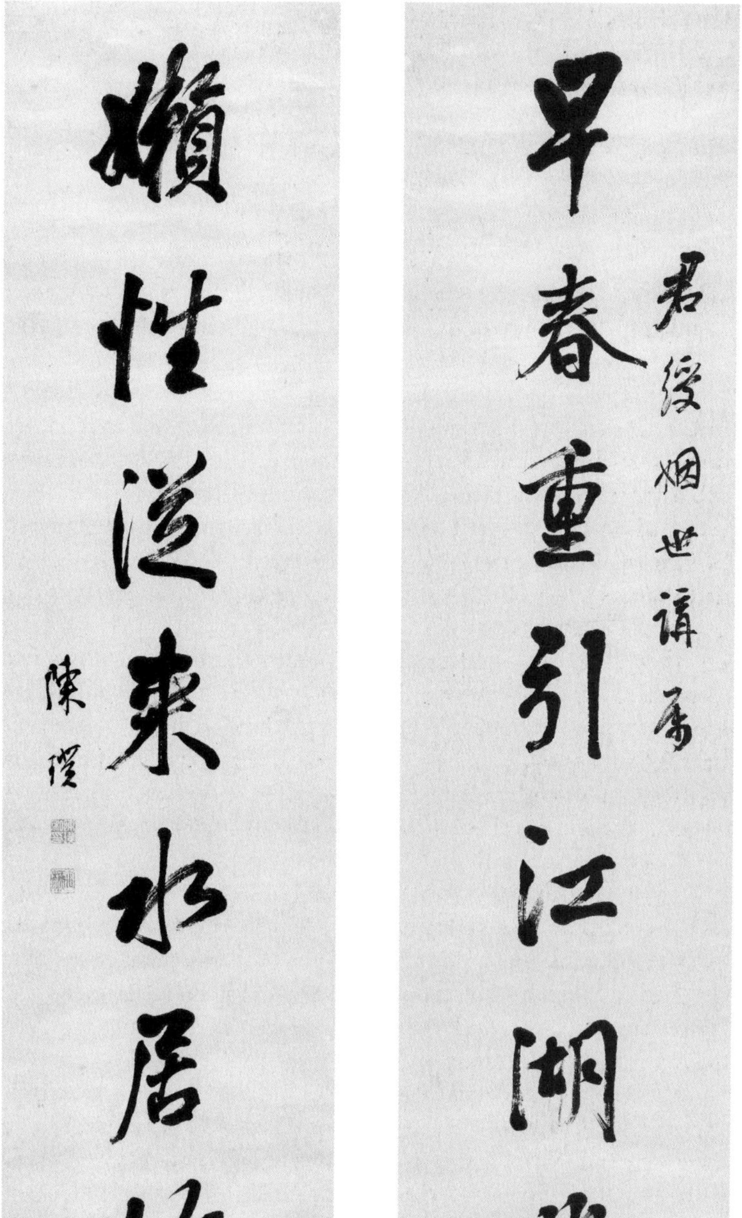

早春重引江湖興
君綬姻世講屬
懶性從來水居竹
陳璞

14 CHEN Pu 陳璞 (1820–1887)

'Comments on painting' in running script 行書畫論

hanging scroll; ink on paper, 64.5 x 138 cm 246.2005

趙大年令穰平遠絕似右丞，秀潤天成，眞宋士大夫畫。此派又傳爲倪雲林。
款識：午垣世兄雅屬。陳璞。
鈐印：陳璞私印。古樵。

Pingyuan created by Zhao Danian [Zhao Lingrang, act 1070–1100] *bears an exact resemblance to that of Youcheng's* [Wang Wei, 701–761] *works; elegant and effortless, it is truly the painting of the Song literati. This style is then bequeathed to Ni Yunlin* [Ni Zan, 1301–74].

Inscription and signature: Written for Wuyuan as he requested. Chen Pu.

The concept *pingyuan* (level-distance perspective) is defined as looking from a place in the foreground over a far distance across a flat landscape. Developed by Guo Xi (c1010–90) of the Song dynasty, it is one of the three classic perspectives of traditional landscape painting which were standardised during the Tang dynasty. Zhao Lingrang was the eleventh grandson of Emperor Taizu (r960–76), founder of the Song dynasty. His landscape paintings, which are generally small and allude to views of misty rivers, made a mark on the lyrical style of the Southern Song period (1127–1279). Wang Wei was a great poet and painter of the Tang dynasty. His work, displaying an intimacy and quiet melancholy, found great favour among later literati artists. Ni Zan was one of the Four Great Masters of the Yuan period (1279–1368), praised for his landscapes painted with dry brushwork, minimal detail and a free ambience. Yet he was admired not only for the strength and refinement of his artwork, but for his personal character which many aspired to emulate.

Chen Pu was also considered an important painter and poet. Along with Li Jian (1747–1799) and Xie Lansheng (1760–1831), the three were praised as *sanjie* (three outstanding painters) in Guangdong region.

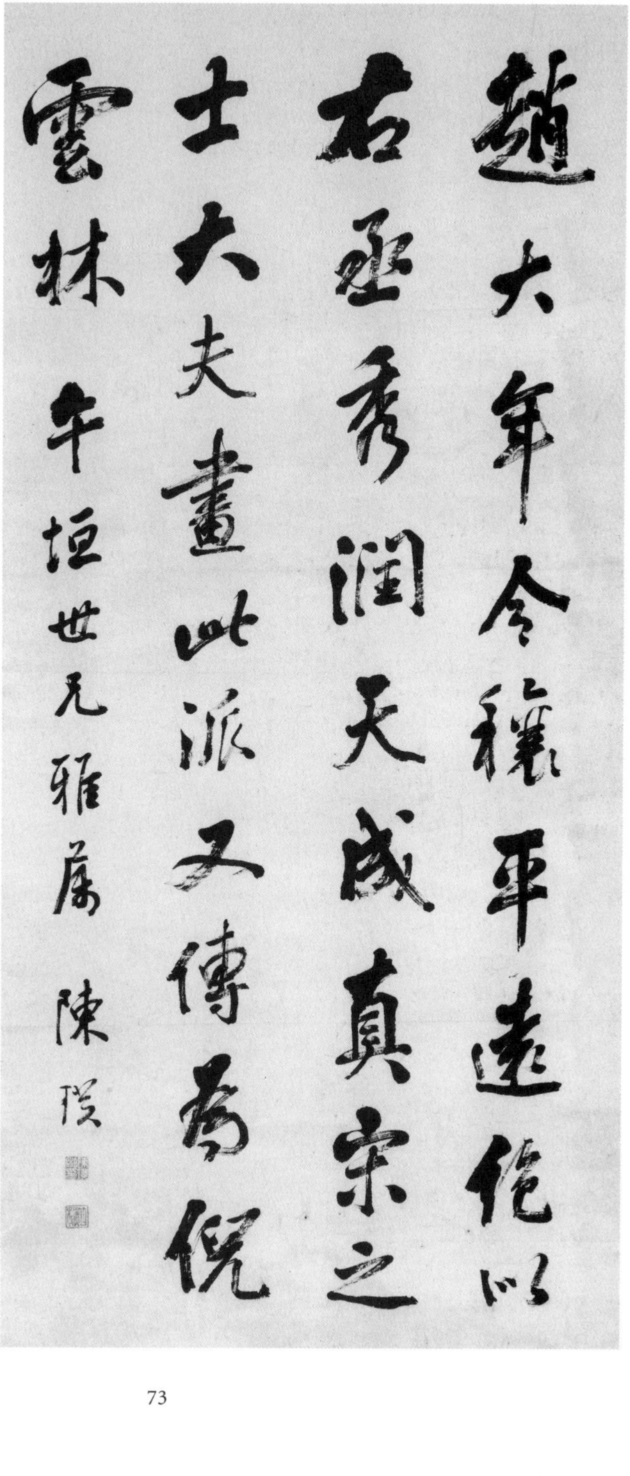
趙大年令穰平遠絕似
右丞秀潤天成真宗之
士大夫畫此派又傳為倪
雲林
年垣世兄雅屬
陳璞

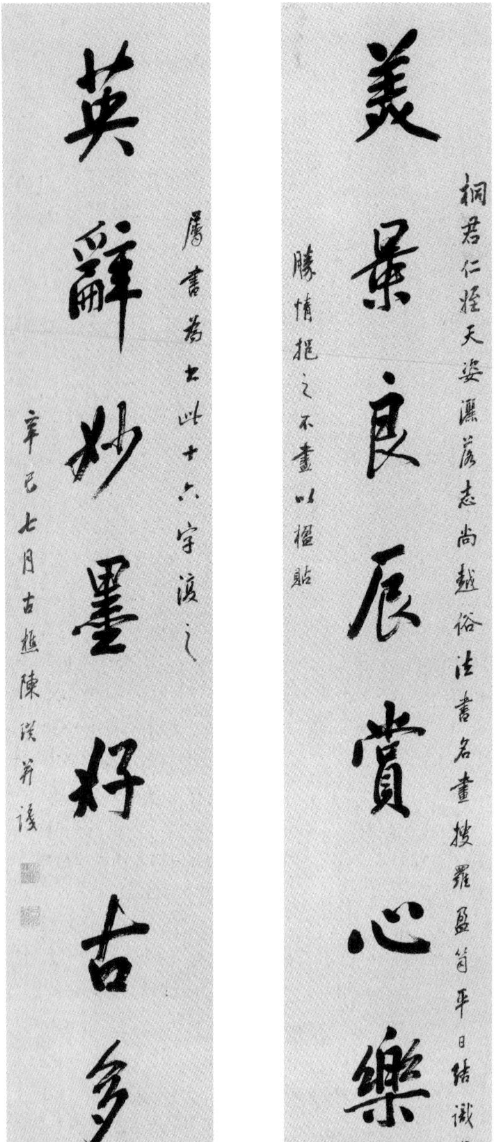
美景良辰賞心樂事
英辭妙墨好古多聞
辛巳七月古樵陳璞并識

15 **CHEN Pu** 陳璞 (1820–1887)

Couplet in running script 行書八言聯 1881

pair of hanging scrolls; ink on paper, 34.3 x 209 cm each 280.2003.a-b

美景良辰賞心樂事；英辭妙墨好古多聞。
款識：桐君仁侄天姿灑落，志尚越俗，法書名畫搜羅盈笥。平日結識名流，雅抱勝情，挹之不盡。以楹貼屬書，爲書此十六字復之。辛巳七月古樵陳璞並識
鈐印：陳璞之印。尺岡歸樵。

A beautiful scene on a bright day; cheerful things delighting the mind;
Illustrious words and excellent brushes; an admirer of antiquity and man of great erudition.

Inscription and signature: My nephew Tongjun has a natural manner; he is a person with lofty aspirations. Over the years he has collected a great many refined calligraphies and paintings. In his lifetime he has been a friend to many celebrities, having his bosom filled with boundless lofty sentiment. He requested I do a couplet for him; so I wrote these sixteen words as a reply. Inscribed by Chen Pu, style name Guqiao, in the seventh moon of the year *xinsi* [1881].

The first line of this couplet was taken from prose written by Xie Lingyun (385–433), an eminent poet of the Southern dynasty, in which he wrote: 'Under heaven, a bright day, a beautiful scene, delights for the mind and cheerful things – to find these four things together is not easy.' Poetic expression was enshrined in popular culture by Tang Xianzu (1550–1616), an esteemed playwright from the Ming dynasty. Tang adapted the words of a song in one of his operas – in this case *The peony pavilion,* composed in the early 17th century, the song being sung by the heroine Du Liniang. The second line appears in Mi Fu's colophon (written in 1087) on a handscroll entitled 'Elegant gathering at western garden', painted by his contemporary Li Gongling (1049–1106).[1] 'Being an admirer of antiquity and a man of great erudition' were the requirements established by Confucius for a pefect gentleman (in *Analects*). Mi Fu used poetic expression to extol the lofty nature of scholars attending that gathering. It was such poetic expression, immersed in literary overtones, which Chen Pu singled out as a compliment to his nephew.

The couplet was written in Chen's later years. His calm style of running script became bolder and more forceful, achieving a marvellous balance of self-expression and calligraphic technique. He used dry brush and swift sweeping strokes to create the effect of 'fly-white' (the rapid sweep of the brush leaving traces of white), thus imparting a roughness and vigour to the form.

1 Mi Fu, 'A note to the painting "Elegant gathering at western garden" 西園雅集圖記'

16 **ZENG Guoquan** 曾國荃 (1824–1890)

Couplet in running script 行書集蘇軾詩七言聯

pair of hanging scrolls; ink on paper, 44.3 x 211.5 cm each 289.2003.a-b

玉芝紫筍生無數；露葉風枝晚自匀。
款識：升階守戊雅正，源甫曾國荃。
鈐印：威毅伯印。青宮少保。

The jade zhi mushrooms and purple bamboo shoots grow profusely;
When evening dew falls, windswept tree branches become calm and neat.

Inscription and signature: For the appraisal of Shengjie, Zeng Guoquan, alias Yuanfu.

The first line of the couplet was taken from a poem written by Su Shi (1037–1101). In a note to the poem, Su tells that he once had a dream in which he went into a garden and saw some serpent-like purple vines growing upon a well. He was told by the owner of the garden that these were *shizhi* (stone fungi). This line describes the scene he saw. The *zhi* (fungus) in traditional Chinese culture combines the marvellous with the immortal and is said to grow and flourish only when the monarch is merciful and humane. The fungus was also a key ingredient in elixirs. The second line of the couplet is from another poem by Su Shi, originally brushed on a fan. Su describes a serene scene in which one could leave behind all disturbing affairs.[1] The ideas of immortality and eremitism are often intermingled in traditional Chinese culture, so the assembling of such poetry would be a literary amusement.

Zeng Guoquan (alias Yuanfu 沅甫, style name Shuchun 叔純) was born into a rich family of landowners in Shuangfeng, Hunan province. In 1855, he passed a special examination and was selected as a candidate (*gongsheng*) to study at the Guozijian Imperial Academy in Beijing. Unfortunately, activities in the capital were disrupted by the rebel movements associated with the Taiping Rebellion (1851–64). Consequently, Zeng joined his celebrated elder brother General Zeng Guofan (1811–72) to help him suppress the rebellion, and like him became a successful military commander. Reverting to civilian employment thereafter, he held various government posts and was honoured with the title of Grand Guardian of the Heir Apparent. After his death, Emperor Guangxu honoured him with the posthumous title of 忠襄 (loyal and supportive).[2]

Zeng's couplet is written in *xingshu* (running script). He preferred to apply ink gracefully, keeping it light in tone, rather than making it dark and weighty. This charm and elegance is in striking contrast to his rough military life. The style of the writing is close to that of the Ming calligrapher Dong Qichang.

1 Su Shi, 'Stone fungi, with a note 石芝, 並引', and 'Written on Shen'gong's fan at the backyard of Guangling 廣陵後園題申公扇子'

2 See *Qing shigao, Biography* 200; Hummel, pp 749–51

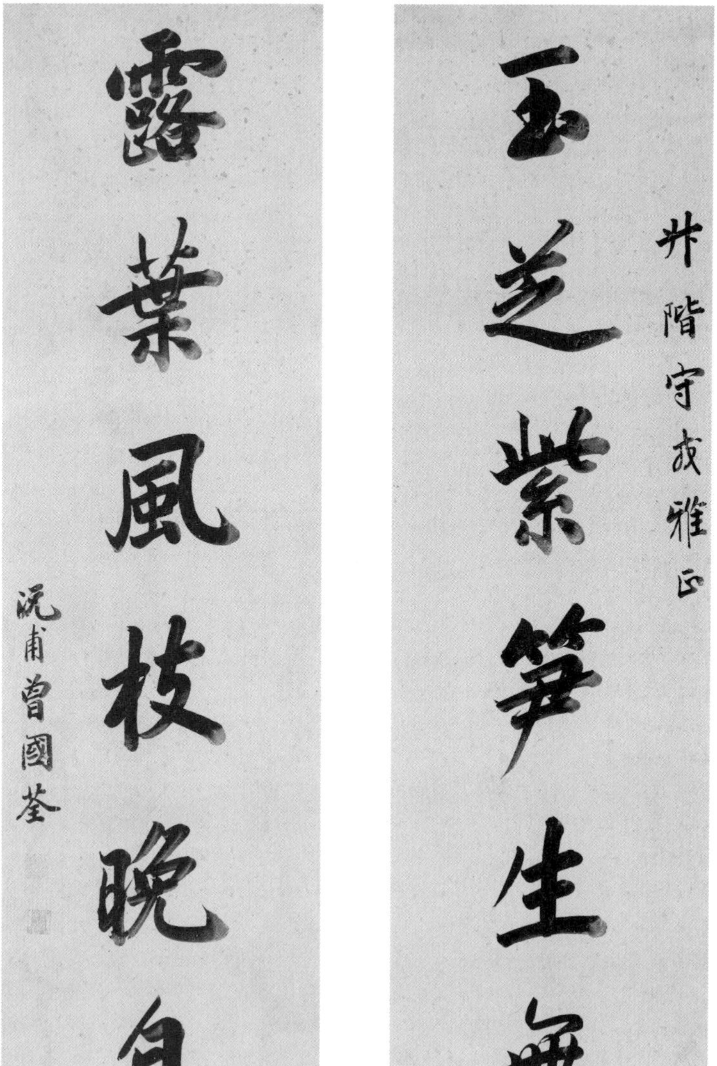

升階守戎雅正
玉芝紫筍生無數
露葉風枝晚自勻
沅甫曾國荃

17 **LU Qiguang** 魯琪光 (1828 – after 1895)

Couplet in running script 行書七言聯

pair of hanging scrolls; ink on paper, 133.7 x 32.2 cm 290.2003.a-b

秀色松筠千載上，奇姿鸞鶴五雲端。
款識：金垣七兄大人雅屬。弟魯琪光。
鈐印：琪光印信。

The luxuriant pine and strong bamboo endure for one thousand years;
The fanciful phoenix and the crane soar above the highest clouds.

Inscription and signature: Written for Jinyuan as he requested. Lu Qiguang.

In traditional Chinese culture, the pine tree and bamboo along with other plants often form emblems of Confucian virtue – this grouping of exemplary plants endures when all others have succumbed. Their enduring qualities in turn also make them conventional symbols of longevity. Unlike the pine and bamboo whose symbolism derives from their natural quality, the allegory of phoenix and crane comes from their association with myth and religion. Both were considered heavenly birds. While the appearance of a phoenix may mark the beginning of a new era of peaceful and prosperous times, the crane represents the travel vehicle of the celestial being. Combining all these motifs together, the allusion of the couplet goes beyond Confucian moral symbolism to become an evocation of the otherworldly or immortal.

Lu Qiguang (alias Zhiyou 芝友) was a native of Nanfeng in Jiangxi province. He passed the imperial civil service examination in 1868 and was granted the *jinshi* degree. He served in several posts of the imperial government, including magistrate of Jinan prefecture. Lu developed his own brisk and well-knit style by modelling himself on the calligraphy masters of the Jin dynasty. The pleasant and elegant quality of his calligraphy is in tune with the spirit of Dong Qichang and Zhao Mengfu. Accordingly his calligraphy was in high demand, and his house was always filled with requests from friends and admirers for his works. Skilled in running script, he could brush dozens of pieces a day without getting bored.[1]

1 In Tao Sheyuan 陶涉園 *Zhaodao mingren chidu xiaozhuan xuji* 昭代名人尺牘續集

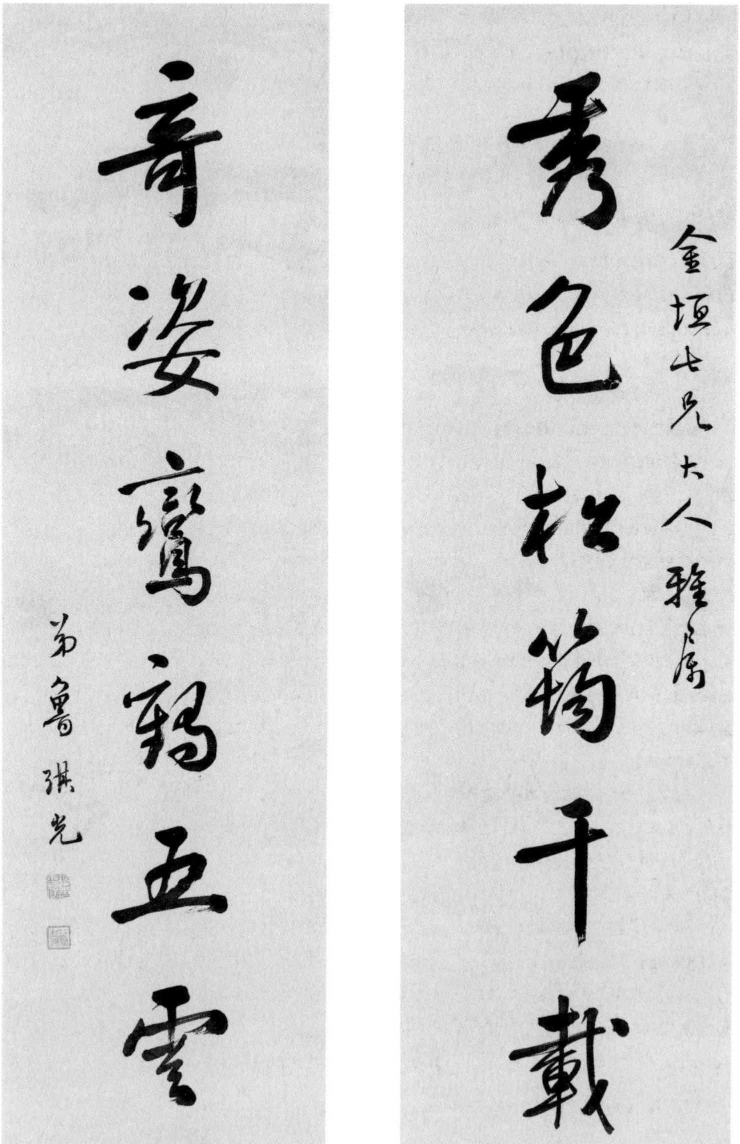
金垣七兄大人雅屬
秀色松筠千載上
奇姿鸞鶴五雲端
弟魯琪光

18 **LI Hongwen** 李鴻文 (1832–1885)

Couplet in running script 行書集李商隱、蘇軾詩七言聯 1876

pair of hanging scrolls; ink on paper, 38.2 x 154.5 cm each 313.2003.a-b

憶事懷人兼得句；引盃看劍自生風。
款識：漢泉仁兄法正。丙子秋日，李鴻文。
鈐印：李鴻文印。

Recalling the past and thinking of friends, that is also an inspiration for poetry;
Holding up a cup while gazing at a sword, which arouses a heroic spirit.

Inscription and signature: Written for the appraisal of Hanquan, in autumn of the year of *bingzi* [1876] by Li Hongwen.

The couplet is drawn from two poems by Li Shangying (c813–c858) of the Tang and Su Shi of the Northern Song respectively.[1] 'Thinking of old times and friends' is a ubiquitous theme in Chinese poetry, and is particularly popular among those poets labelled with the style known as *wanyue* (delicate restraint), to which Li is assigned. On the other hand, Su Shi is the foremost poet of the *haofang* (unrestrained and masculine) school, which cultivated an attitude of heroic abandon. While lamenting the past is typical of *wanyue* poets' sentiment, singing the praises of wine and sword, intoxicated with soaring determination, is characteristic of *haofang* poetry. The couplet puts together lines from poems of distinct styles, thus creating a thoughtful tension.

Li Hongwen (alias Yukui 羽逵) was a native of Huazhou, Guangdong province. He gained the *juren* degree in 1867 and had played an important role in raising local militia forces to resist the Nian rebels in 1864. He later taught at several academies in Guangzhou, including Shilong and Wen'guan.

1 Li Shangying, 'Yaozhuan 藥轉'; Su Shi, 'Drinking with Ou Yu and six others 與歐育等六人飲酒'

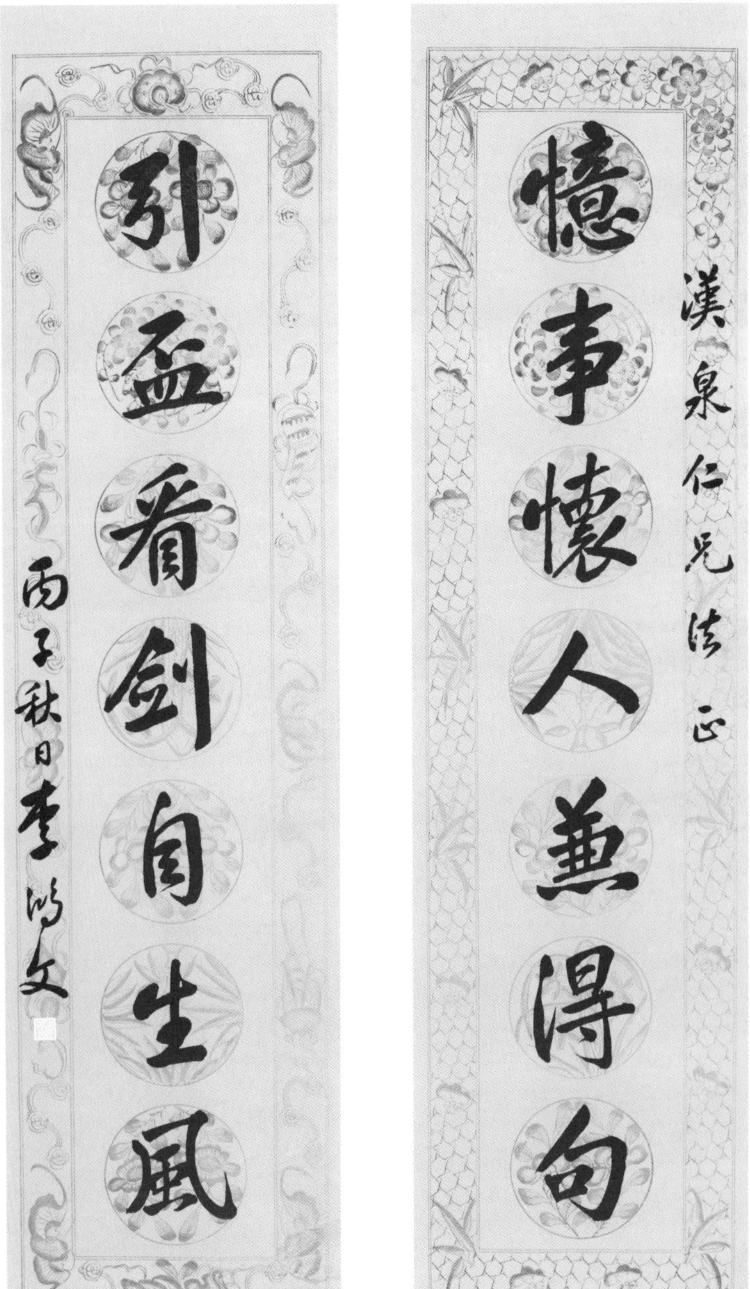

憶事懷人兼得句
漢泉仁兄法正
引盃看劍自生風
丙子秋日李鴻文

19 **LI Wentian** 李文田 (1834–1895)

Couplet in regular script 楷書八言聯

pair of hanging scrolls; ink on paper, 41 x 204.5 cm each 277.2003.a-b

威鳳祥麟瞻其文彩；芝蘭玉樹貽爾子孫。
款識：炤南大兄大人喜鑒。若農。弟李文田。
鈐印：臣李文田。若農。

[Your] *literary talent and grace are as majestic as the phoenix and as auspicious as the unicorn;*
[Your] *descendants will benefit and 'flourish in the courtyard' like magic mushrooms and fragrant orchids.*

Inscription and signature: For the joyful appraisal of Mr Zhaonan. Li Wentian, style name Ruonong.

The expressions 'phoenix feather' and 'unicorn's horn' symbolically hint at the notion of great genius. The references to fungus and orchid in the second line allude to an anecdote about Xie Xuan (343–88), the gifted military strategist and poet of the Eastern Jin dynasty. The story tells of how when Xie was a boy, he was once asked by his uncle what would be the most suitable way to raise children. Xie replied, 'They should be given the opportunity to grow in a courtyard like fungus, orchid or the jade tree'. Xie was implying that just like the evolution of these auspicious plants, the nobility and glory of the family would carry on generation after generation. The grouping of 'fungus, orchid and jade tree' later became the metaphor for gifted children in a family. As such the couplet would be a suitable tribute to congratulate a scholar-official's achievements, both his scholarship and the prosperity brought to the family line. Its visual appeal is enhanced by the material Li used – the red paper with scattered gilding reinforces the auspicious allusions of the poem.

Li Wentian (alias Sheguang 畬光, style name Ruonong 若農) was a native of Shunde in Guangdong. At the age of 26, he received his *jinshi* degree (granted title of *tanhua* – third place) and assumed the position of a compiler at the Hanlin Academy. He served as the educational commissioner in Jiangxi and Zhili (present-day Hebei), as the chief examiner in Jiangsu and Zhejiang, vice-president of the Board of Ceremonies and during his years of absence from the court (having taken leave to look after his ill mother), he taught in Guangzhou. His students included Cai Yuanpei (1868–1940), the eminent educator and former chancellor of Peking University.[1]

Li was also an eminent historian. His outstanding scholarship included his research into Mongolian history and the geography of north-western China. He was also recognised during his time as an important scholar in the stele studies (*beixue*) movement. During the late Qing, *beixue* overshadowed the previously prevalent *tiexue* which was based on the study of classical calligraphy models. Scholar-calligraphers did not only collect, study and catalogue inscriptions taken from stone carvings of the Northern Wei, but also adopted and merged the elements of these calligraphies into their own calligraphic practice. Li Wentian was one of the most influential advocates of the Northern Wei stele style, condemning the more conventional style of *tiexue*. Li himself had an extensive collection of stele rubbings from the Qin to the Yuan dynasties period (3rd BCE–14th centuries). His assiduous absorption of early stele models produced a very distinctive style in the history of Chinese calligraphy, as demonstrated in this couplet.

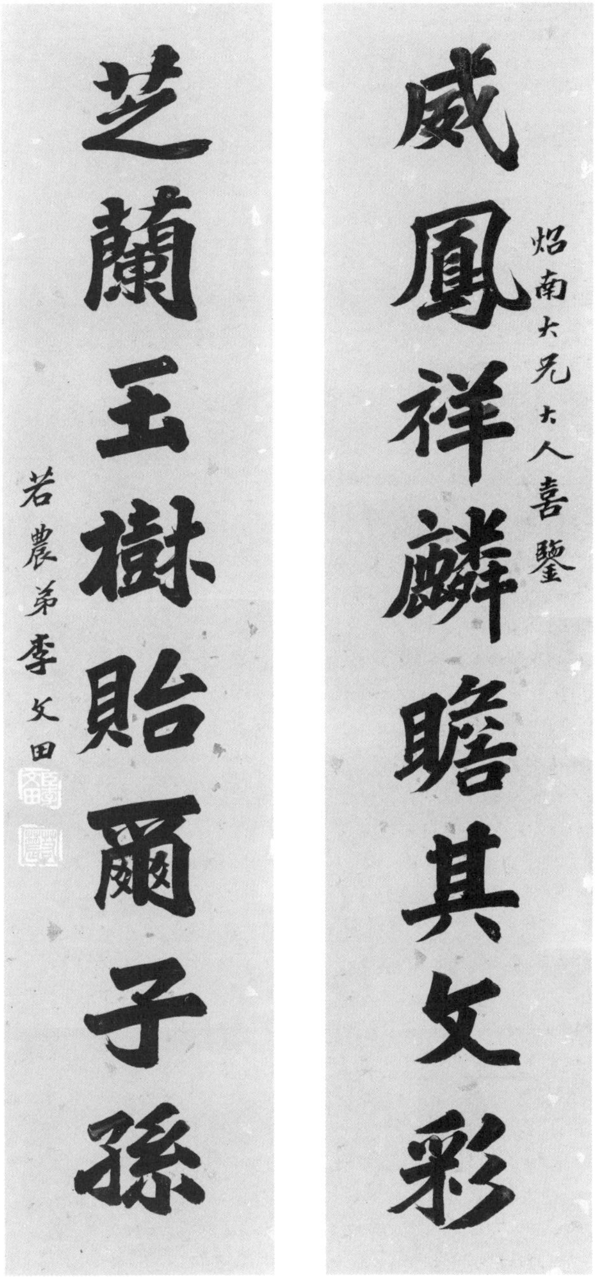

1 See *Qing shigao*, *Biography* 228; Hummel, pp. 494–95

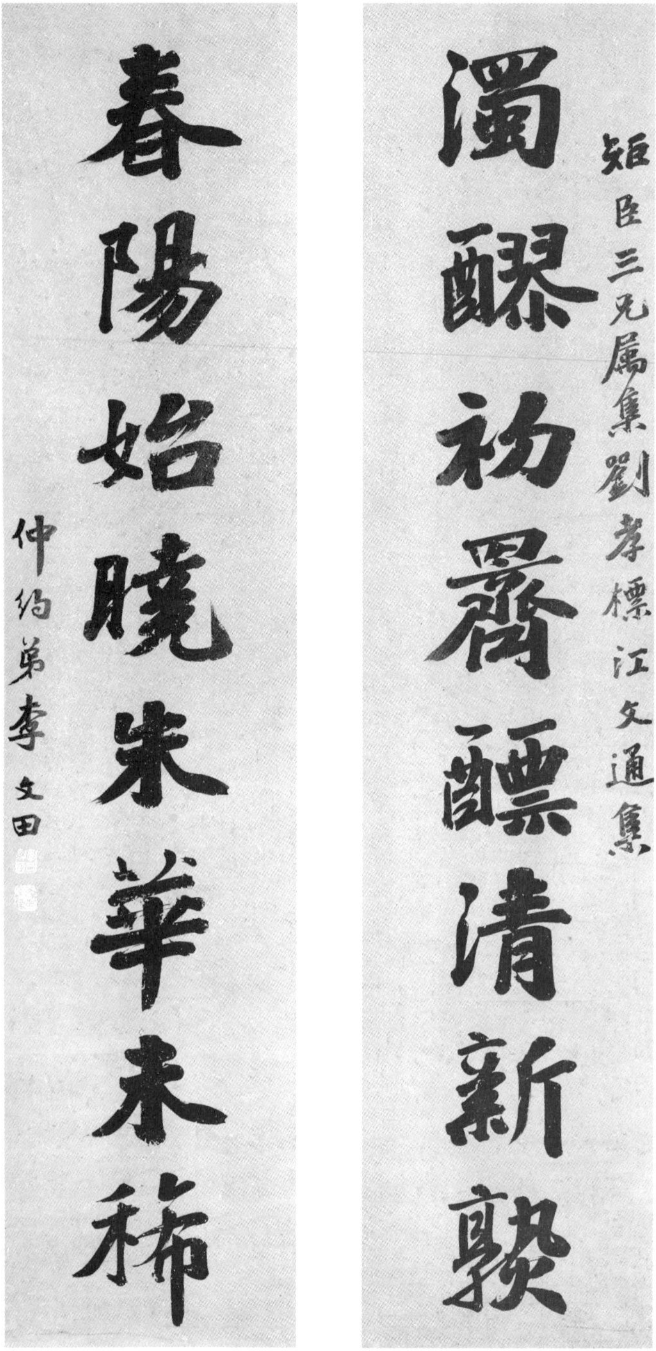
濁醁初爵醥清新熟
矩臣三兄屬集劉孝標江文通集
春陽始曉朱華未稀
仲約弟李文田

20 LI Wentian 李文田 (1834–1895)

Couplet in regular script 楷書集劉孝標、江淹詩八言聯

pair of hanging scrolls; ink on paper, 40.1 x 174.5 cm each 278.2003.a-b

濁醪初齊,醥清新熟；春陽始曉,朱華未稀。
款識：矩臣三兄屬，集劉孝標江文通集。仲約弟李文田。
鈐印：李氏仲約。文田之印。

The unfiltered wine is ready to drink, and the decanted wine is being warmed;
The spring is just beginning, and the flowers are blossoming.

Inscription and signature: Composed for Juchen as he requested. Assembling poems from writings by Liu Xiaobiao and Jiang Wentong. Li Wentian, alias Zhongyue.

The first line was taken from Liu Xiaobiao's (462–521) annotation on *Shishuo xinyu* (New account of tales of the world) by Liu Yiqing (403–44), where the author rather idealistically describes the sweetness and rewards of peasant life: carefree gatherings at tree groves during the slow season, drinking, chatting and enjoying nature.[1] The second line is derived from a poetic prose composed by Jiang Yan (444–505) and portrays the magnificent scenery of Tuyuan, a vast landscaped garden built in Kaifeng by Prince Liu Wu, son of the Han dynasty emperor Xiaowen (r179–57 BCE), where he often hosted sumptuous feasts.[2] The unity of opposites between the two lines – the enjoyment of nature and the lives of people from different classes – gives the couplet a contemplative quality.

As with the previous couplet, the work is written in regular script. The execution of this script in Li Wentian's hand, however, involved techniques of brush manipulation that were adapted from other script types. Unlike the common form of regular script, which is slender and symmetrical, Li's writing absorbed bold lines, energetic hook strokes and a strongly horizontal emphasis to create the manner of writing seen in these two couplets. Li was an eminent scholar of epigraphy and a collector of rubbings of inscriptions taken from bronzes and stele, and the great influence of antique writing in his calligraphy is obvious. More specifically, his calligraphy absorbed the spirit and character of the Northern Wei stele script, which focused on strength and simplicity. On the basis of classical calligraphy models such as that of Ouyang Xun (557–641) of the Tang dynasty, yet drawing on the structural principles of the Northern Wei style of script, Li created a new form of regular script that rapidly became the model for followers, particularly in the Guangdong region.

1 See Fang Xuanling (Tang), *Jinshu* (History of the Jin dynasty), Zhonghua Press, Bejing, 1974, 'Biography of Xie An', and Liu Yiqing (420–79), *Shishuo xinyu*, Guji Press, Shanghai, 1993, in *yanyu* 言語 section
2 Jiang Yan, 'A descriptive prose on Duke Liang's Tuyuan 梁王兔園賦', in Xu Jian (8th century), *Chuxue ji* 初學記, *juan* 24

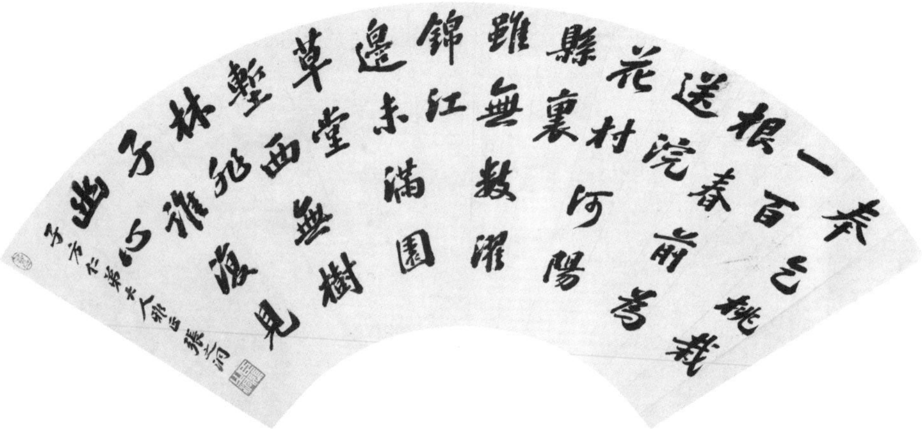

21 **ZHANG Zhidong** 張之洞 (1837–1909)

Du Fu's poem in running script 行書杜甫詩

fan; ink on paper, 40.8 x 69.5 cm 301.2003

奉乞桃栽一百根，春前爲送浣花村。河陽縣裏雖無數，濯錦江邊未滿園。草堂塹西無樹林，非子誰複見幽心。

款識：子方仁弟大人雅正。張之洞。

鈐印：臣張之洞。

I made a request for a hundred peach seedlings,
Before the spring, to be delivered to Huanhua village.
Once upon a time, spring petals flew throughout Heyang city
But here, at the side of Zhuojin River, spring buds have not yet filled the entire garden!
Beyond the moat of the thatched cottage, there are no trees,
Who could experience my exquisite feeling, except you?

Inscription and signature: Written for the appraisal of Zifang. Zhang Zhidong.

This calligraphy is composed of lines from two poems by the famous Tang dynasty poet Du Fu (712–70), written for a friend and executed on a fan. In the year 759, constrained by poverty and social upheaval, Du Fu moved from Gansu province to the outskirts of Chengdu in Sichuan, and built a thatched hut alongside Huanhuaxi (Flower Washing Brook). In order to make the surroundings more lush and green, he made requests to the county magistrate for peach seedlings (first poem), and to a friend for alder seedlings (second poem).[1] The name Heyang which he mentions alludes to the gifted poet of the Western Jin dynasty, Pan Yue (247–300), who during his time as the magistrate of Heyang (in Henan) turned the county into a peach garden! In traditional China, sustaining fertile grounds was considered an admirable deed for a local official, and the expression 'planting trees' was a metaphor for professional training: these thoughts might have been on Zhang Zhidong's mind when he wrote the poems on the fan for a friend – possibly a fellow official.

Zhang Zhidong (alias Xiaoda 孝達, style name Xiangtao 香濤), younger brother of Zhang Zhiwan, was a native of Napi in Hebei province. He gained his *jinshi* degree in 1863, attaining third place (*tanhua*). He was appointed literary chancellor for Sichuan in 1873, became sub-reader of the Hanlin in 1880, and secretary in the Grand Secretariat in 1881. In 1882, he was made governor of Shanxi province. In 1884, he became viceroy of Guangdong and Guangxi, then governor of Hubei, viceroy of Jiangsu and Zhejiang, minister for commerce and minister of the State Council. One of the foremost reformers of his time, Zhang Zhidong promoted modernisation in the economy, education, transportation and the military during the last years of the Qing dynasty. He took charge of the construction of the Hanyang steel plant, then the largest of its kind in Asia, and the Hubei Firearms Factory. He also founded a mint, tanneries, tile and silk factories, and paper, cotton and wool mills. He helped build a railway line from Hankou in Hubei that extended towards the vicinity of Beijing. Concerned with rejuvenating and modernising China, he searched for ways that would allow the country to survive in a modern world and would accommodate Western knowledge but preserve traditional ways.[2]

In calligraphy, Zhang was a devout follower of the calligraphy style of Su Shi (1037–1101), the eminent scholar and one of the four great Northern Song calligraphers. Like Su he was an expert in *xingshu* (running script). The calligraphy was executed with momentum; the bold vertical line but relatively thinner horizontal stroke, and the slightly horizontal emphasis, are all characteristics of Zhang's script.

1 Du Fu, 'Requests to Xiao Baming's mansion for peach seedlings 蕭八明府實處覓桃栽'; 'Requests to He Yong for alder seedlings 憑何十一少府邕覓木栽'
2 See *Qing shigao*, *Biography* 224; Hummel, pp 27–31

22 **LU Runxiang** 陸潤庠 (1841–1915)

Couplet in running script 行書八言聯

pair of hanging scrolls; ink on paper, 170 x 34.3 cm each

疏仡因提七緯能紀；蒼舒隤敳八愷同生。
款識：子信仁兄雅屬，鳳石陸潤庠。
鈐印：陸潤庠。太傅銜太保。

[Throughout the eras of] *Shuyi and Yinti, seven classics remain guiding principles; Cangshu and Tuizhu* [together with others], *eight sages were born in the same era.*

Inscription and signature: Written at the request of Zixing. Lu Runxiang, alias Fengshi.

According to a Chinese chronology written in the Han dynasty, there spanned 2 260 000 years from the beginning of history till the time of Confucius, consisting of 10 eras that included the Yinti (seventh) and Shuyi (tenth) eras mentioned in the couplet. During Zhuanxu's reign, there were Eight Worthies who assisted him in ruling the country, including Cangshu and Tuizhu. The late Han Confucianists considered that the 10 eras shaped *jing* (latitude) or a continuous history; while the seven major Confucian classics formed *wei* (longitude).[1] The couplet is a summary of this historiography that blended together legends with the ideas of late Han Confucianism.

Lu Runxiang (alias Fengshi 鳳石, style name Shisa 石灑) was a native of modern-day Suzhou, Jiangsu province. In 1874, he qualified in the highest imperial examination, taking first place among 337 recipients of the *jinshi* degree, and was granted the crowning honour of *zhuangyuan*. With an outstanding academic background, Lu climbed rapidly up the bureaucratic ladder: he was required to serve at the Imperial Study then became libationer of the Imperial Academy. In 1898 he was promoted to sub-chancellor of the Grand Secretariat, then deputy-minister of the Ministry of Ceremonies, president of the Censorate, and minister of the Ministry of Works. In 1909, when Puyi came to the throne, he was appointed the young emperor's tutor. He was canonised as *wenduan* (cultivated and upright) upon his death.[2]

Lu Runxiang's accomplishments in calligraphy were made within the tradition of *tiexue* (study of classical calligraphy models), a tradition derived from the graceful art of Wang Xizhi. His running script reflects the style known as 'foundation of Ou, surface of Zhao'. Lu's personality found expression in his well-disciplined calligraphy, which seemed to reflect his conservative view on political affairs. During the last years of the Qing dynasty, he was in strong opposition to the reformers' attempts to establish a constitutional monarchy in China.

1 In *Guangya* 廣雅, chapter of *Han lizhi* 漢歷志
2 See *Qing shigao, Biography* 259; Hummel, pp 360–61

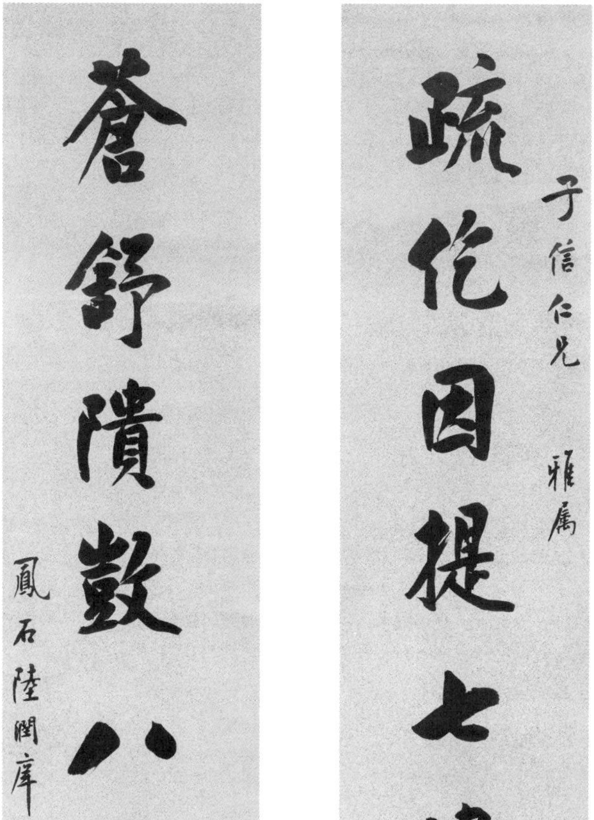
疏佗因提七緯能紀
子信仁兄雅屬
蒼舒隤敳八愷同升
鳳石陸潤庠

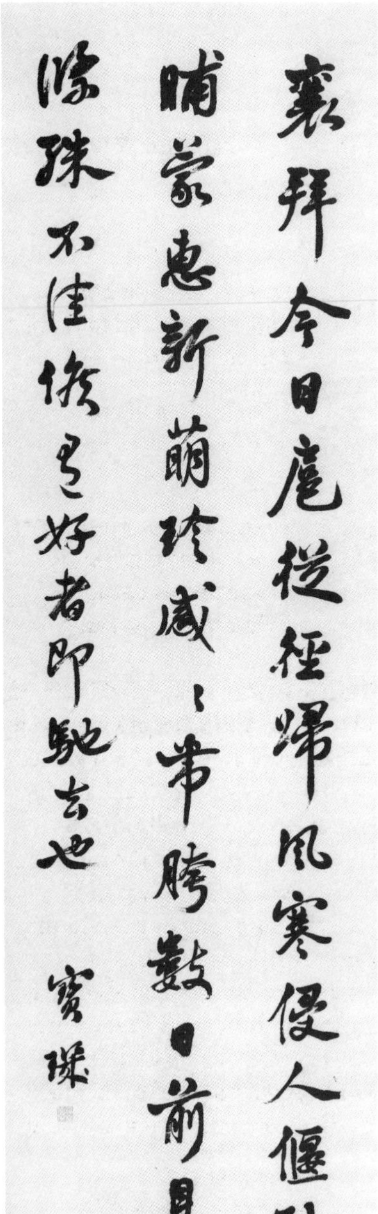

曩拜令日庵從經歸風寒侵人偃臥至
晡蒙惠新萌琖感ㄟ常騰數日前見數
隊珠不佳倘是好者即馳去也

寶琛

23 **QIN Baoji** 秦寶璣 (?–1882)

Copy of a personal letter in running script 行書臨尺牘

hanging scroll; ink on paper, 166.1x 46 cm 304.2003

襄拜：今日扈從徑歸，風寒侵人，偃臥至晡。蒙惠新萌，珍感感。帶胯數日前見數條，殊不佳，候有好者，即馳去也。
款識：寶璣。
鈐印：秦寶璣印。

Xiang gives a polite response: Today my whole retinue returned [to their own homes]. *A chill in the air struck, and I was in bed till late afternoon. I am very grateful to you for the new tea you sent me. As for the belt, I did see a few some days ago, yet none of them were exceptional. If I find a good one, I shall inform you immediately.*

Inscription and signature: Baoji.

Qin Baoji (alias Yaochen 姚臣, style name Qianshu 潛叔) was a native of present day Wuxi in Jiangsu province. In 1867 he passed the prefecture level of the civil service examination and was granted the *xiucai* degree. He was then selected as a student to study at the Imperial Academy. Qin excelled in poetry and had published an anthology of his own poems.[1]

The calligraphy is a *lin* (close copy) of an unidentified earlier master's *chidu* 尺牘 (personal letter). Before the invention of paper, bamboo strip and slabs of wood were used to write messages on. Originally, during the Han dynasty, a regular sized wood slab, known as a *chidu*, was used to write government decrees. Later the term *chidu* came to mean 'personal letter'. It is evident that the source for calligraphy during the Jin dynasty – the period when the *tiexue* tradition was shaped – relied mainly on surviving handwritten letters by calligraphers of the time. During this period correspondence between private persons became more and more important among scholars. The earliest extant calligraphic work by a famous calligrapher is a letter written by Lu Ji (261–303) of the Western Jin, now known as *Pingfu tie* 平復帖. The most important works by another calligrapher, Wang Xizhi, come to us in the form of letters and notes. Unlike other formal writing, these personal letters written in a more casual and informal style of running or cursive script with a carefree manner, are greatly treasured and are taken to be at the heart of the *tiexue* tradition: the study of classical calligraphy models.

1 See Dou Zhen 竇鎮, *Qingchao shuhuajia bilu* 清朝書畫家筆錄 (Records of colligraphers and painters of the Qing period)

24 **XU Shichang** 徐世昌 (1855–1939)

Lu You's poems in cursive script 草書陸遊絕句二首 1929

hanging scroll; ink on paper, 90.0 x 37.1 cm 298.2003

小市易散無人行，茫茫湖橋惟月明。老夫解酲不用酒，自有千頃菰蒲聲。
七月湖中風露新，臨流閑照白綸巾。荷花折盡渾閒事，老卻蓴絲最惱人。
款識：己巳夏五月石心山人。
鈐印：徐世昌印。鞠人長壽。

With no trace of men, the market readily disperses,
Now only the moon sheds a hazy light on the lake bridge.
To recover from a hangover the old man doesn't need wine,
There are sounds of a thousand wild reeds.

In July the wind and dew from the lake are new,
At leisure I look into the mirror-like water to see my white headwear.
Although the disappearance of lotus is not my concern,
It still stirs melancholy when the waterweeds wither up.

Inscription and signature: Written in the summer, fifth moon of the year *jisi* [1929] by Shixin shanren.

Xu Shichang (alias Puwu 菿五, style name Juren 菊人) was a prominent politician during the Republican period. A native of Tianjing, he was born in Henan, received his *jinshi* degree in 1886, and became a compiler at the Hanlin Academy. He held a series of senior positions in the Qing court, including deputy minister of the Ministry of War, minister of the State Council, minister of police, and viceroy of Manchuria. When China became a republic, Xu was appointed as state secretary, and in 1918 he became president of the Republic of China. In 1922 he retired to Tianjing, and spent the rest of his life painting and doing calligraphy.

This calligraphy was done during his later years in retirement, and is composed of two poems by the famous Southern Song dynasty poet Lu You (1125–1210).[1] Lu had an unsuccessful official career and soon retired in frustration, returning to his home town of Shaoxing. He went on to be regarded as one of the greatest poets in Chinese literary history. The two poems, written during his absence from the court, express his loneliness and an acute awareness of the passing of time. It was such melancholy sentiments that struck a responsive chord in Xu's consciousness.

Xu Shichang was an advocate of the conventional style of *tiexue*, based on the study of classical calligraphy models. He uses his running script to great advantage, displaying a carefree grace while maintaining the complexity of the style.

1 Lu You, 'Two poems written during boating on the lake in late summer and early autumn in the year *yichou* 乙丑夏秋之交小舟早晚往來湖中絕句'

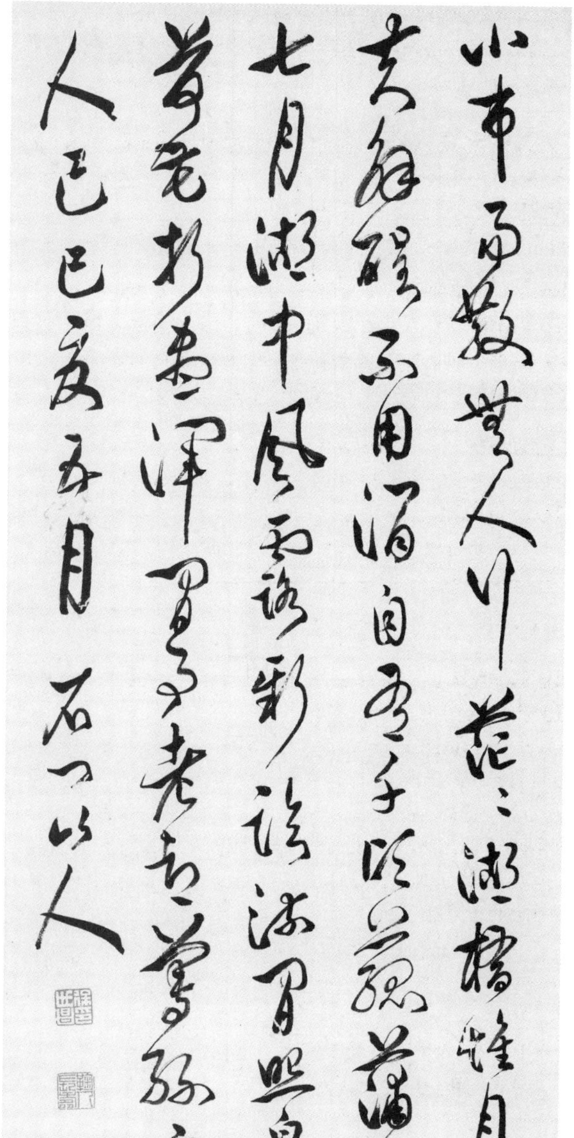

25 CHEN Botao 陳伯陶 (1855–1939)

Mi Fu's letter in running script 行書米芾尺牘

four hanging scrolls; ink on paper, 39.5 x 192.5cm each 291.2003.a-d

[第一聯] 環居桐柳椿杉百十本，以糞植之。今十年，皆垂陰一畝，眞一畝之居也。[第二聯] 四月末，上皇山樵人以異石告。遂視之，八十一穴，大如椀，小容指，制在淮 [第三聯] 山一品之上。百夫運致寶晉桐杉之間。五月望，甘露滿石次，林木焦葦，[第四聯] 莫不霑，潔白如玉珠。郡中圖去，至今未止。
款識：達初三兄雅屬。陳伯陶。
鈐印：伯陶之印。梅花村主人。

The residence is encircled by hundreds of wutong [Chinese parasol trees], *willows, Chinese toons and China firs. They were fertilised with manure, so after ten years they grew into an enormous shady shelter; truly it could be called 'a shaded abode'. During the late fourth moon, the woodcutter of Mount Shanghuang came to tell me there was an unusual rock. So I went there to have a look. The rock had eighty-one holes – the largest one resembled a bowl and the smallest one could only fit a finger. Its quality and features were superb. I employed a hundred workers to carry the rock down* [the mountain] *and relocated it in among the trees* [surrounding my abode]. *On the 15th day of the 5th moon, pleasant dews which were as white as jade pearls, fell and covered the rock, trees and reeds. The district* [officials] *were trying to take it for themselves, and even to this day they still have not given up.*

Inscription and signature: Written for Dachu as he requested, Chen Botao.

Chen Botao (alias Xianghua 象華, style name Zili 子礪) was a native of Dongguan in Guangdong province. At the age of 25, he took first place in the prefecture civil service examination, and in 1892 passed the metropolitan examination (*tanhua* 探花, third place) and was granted the position of compiler at the Hanlin Academy.[1] He was appointed the chief examiner for provincial examinations in Yunnan, Guizhou and Shandong. In 1906, he was sent by the court to Japan to investigate the Japanese education system. On his return, he was appointed educational administrator for Jiangsu province, and then deputy governor of the province. He retired to Guangdong in 1910, but in the following year when the republican revolution occurred, moved to Hong Kong and spent the rest of his life there devoting himself to scholarly research and calligraphy. A number of his remaining extant calligraphies are engraved on shrines, pavilions and even hospitals in the regions of Guangdong and Hong Kong.

Chen's composition in these four hanging scrolls is taken from a letter written by the renowned Song dynasty painter and calligrapher Mi Fu (1051–1107), in which Mi, in a graceful and effortless style of running script, portrayed his charming residence at Dantu in present-day Jiangsu province. A comparison of the two works reveals that Chen had copied Mi's style closely. In China, the traditional and most effective way of learning and practising calligraphy comprises a basic step: the *lin* (close copy), in which a novice tries to reproduce an original work as meticulously as possible without the aid of tracing or mechanical means. By copying the model calligraphy, a practitioner learns to recognise structure, patterns and the style of the past masters. The practitioner then writes independently, developing his own style. Since Mi Fu was regarded as one of the most brilliantly inventive calligraphers in Chinese history, his works were mostly copied by those learning calligraphy. Like many established calligraphers, Chen Botao not only learnt his skill from his teachers Chen Li and Li Wentian, but also from a wide range of calligraphers of the past.

1 Hanlin Academy was an elite scholarly institution at court that performed secretarial, archival and literary tasks for the court and established the official interpretations of the Confucian Classics. By the time of the Qing dynasty, admittance was granted only to those who did exceptionally well in the *jinshi* examination. Hanlin scholars functioned as the emperor's close advisers and confidential secretaries

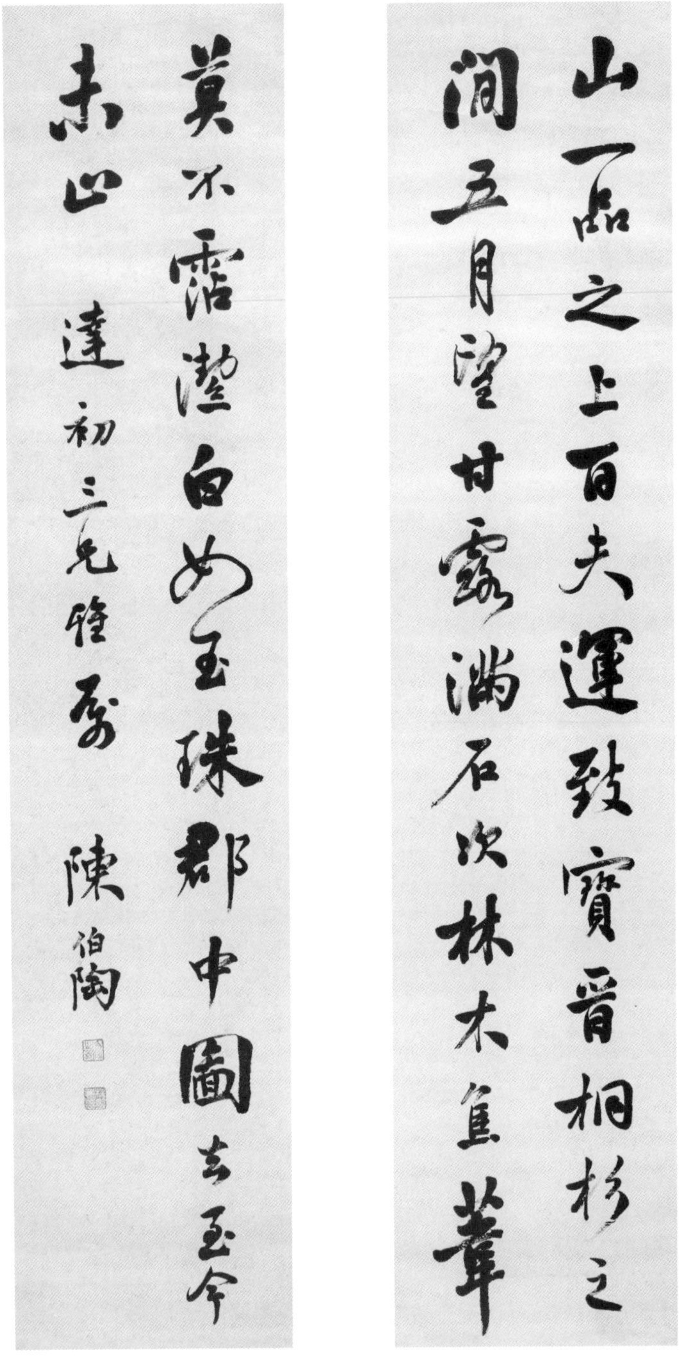
山頂品之上百夫運致寶晉相杉之
間五月望甘露滿石次林木盡華
莫不露澄白如玉珠郡中圖志至今
未
達初三兄雅屬
陳伯陶

環居桐柳椿杉百十本以蕉植之今
十年皆垂蔭一畝真一畝之居也
四月末上皇山樵人以異石告遂
視之八十一穴大如椀小容指製在淮

26 **XU Qi** 徐琪 (c1859 – after 1900)

Couplet in running script 行書集《易林》八言聯 1882

pair of hanging scrolls; ink on paper, 34 x 171cm each 248.2005.a-b

伯歌季舞，燕樂以喜；左酒右漿，與福相迎。
款識：壬午冬日集易林語。花農徐琪。
鈐印：臣徐琪印。庚辰翰林。雙桂廔藏。

The elder sing, the younger dance, everyone is full of happiness and joy;
Carrying wine on the left, tart drink on the right, we greet our fortune.

Inscription and signature: Verse assembled from the *Yilin* in the winter of the year *renwu* [1882] by Xu Qi, alias Huanong.

The couplet was made up of poetry taken from the *Yilin* (Forest of changes), written by Jiao Gan in the 3rd century BCE. Jiao's text is a creative interpretation of the *Yijing* (or *I Ching*, 'Classics of change'), the oldest of the Chinese classic texts describing a system of divination and philosophy centred around the ideas of balance through opposites and acceptance of change. The *Yilin* expands the *Yijing*'s 64 changes into 4096 possible variations, each interpreted by a verse. Taken from two separate verses describing the happiness felt at a family gathering, this couplet would be suitably displayed for a festive occasion.

Xu Qi (alias Huanong 花農) grew up in a prestigious family of scholar-officials in Hangzhou. He obtained the *jinshi* degree in the year of *gengcheng* (1880), a fact also revealed in one of his seals stamped on the couplet. Thus from his great grandfather Xu Chao to himself, the family contributed six *jinshi* and members to the Imperial Hanlin Academy. Xu held various administrative appointments, including Guangdong provincial director of education, junior vice-minister for the Ministry of War, and sub-chancellor of the Grand Secretariat. His graceful calligraphy is seen in many public places in Guangdong and Hangzhou. One example is at a Buddhist temple site called Longqiutan in Lanzhou, Guangdong, where his huge running script of Tang poet Han Yu's (768–824) poem is carved on the side of a cliff.

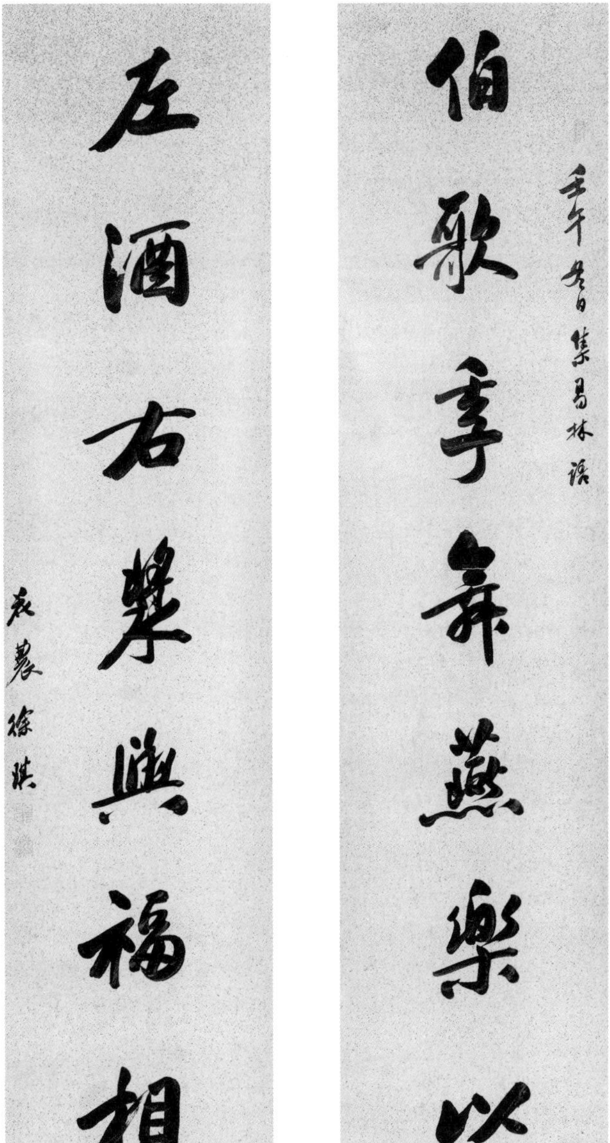
伯歌季舞燕樂以喜
壬午春日集易林語
左酒右漿與福相迎
花農徐琪

27 **ZHENG Xiaoxu** 鄭孝胥 (1860–1938)

Citation in clerical script from the Fan Min Stele 隸書臨《巴郡太守樊敏碑》

hanging scroll; ink on paper, 166.1 x 45.2 cm 299.2003

濯冕題剛，傑立忠謇，有夷史之直，卓密之風。鄉黨見歸，察孝除郎。
款識：臨巴郡太守樊敏碑。孝胥。
鈐印：鄭孝胥印。蘇戡。

[Fan Min is a man of] *outstanding qualities. He is loyal and outspoken; he has the righteousness of an impartial historian, and a distinguished character. Fellow villagers all came and pledged their allegiance to him. He was recommended for his filial piety, and the court conferred on him an official position.*

Inscription and signature: A close copy of the inscription engraved on the Monument of Fan Min, governor of Ba prefecture.

Zheng Xiaoxu (alias Taiyi 太夷, style name Su Kan 蘇戡) was a native of present-day Fuzhou in Fujiang. In 1882 he took the provincial level civil service degree to become a *juren*. He was appointed secretary of the Grand Secretariat in 1891, and went to Japan to work as secretary to the Chinese Embassy in Tokyo; the following year he was promoted to consul general in Kobe then in Osaka. On returning to China, he held senior positions at the Yamen of Foreign Affairs, and was in charge of building the southern section of the railway from Beijing to Hankou. In 1911 he was appointed treasurer in Hunan province. After the fall of the Qing dynasty, he retired to Shanghai, dedicating himself to poetry and calligraphy. The major turning point of his life was his appointment in 1935 as 'prime minister' of Manchukuo (a Japanese puppet-state) by Puyi, the last emperor of China. In spite of his outstanding accomplishments in calligraphy and poetry (he was the leader of a poetry school called *tong guang ti* 同光體), Zheng's role in the puppet government during the Japanese occupation has overshadowed his fame in literature and art.

The calligraphy is a close copy of a segment taken from an inscription carved on a monument from the Eastern Han dynasty (25–220 CE). The stele was erected in 205 CE to commemorate Fan Min, the deceased governor of Ba prefecture (present-day eastern Sichuan). It is considered one of the best preserved examples of clerical script, and has for centuries been the model from which to copy. Clerical script developed from small seal script of the first century BCE, but reached its peak period of usage during the Eastern Han. For hundreds of years, before the mid 18th century, the graceful art of Wang Xizhi had been accepted as the foremost example of Chinese calligraphic style. A large circle of scholars and calligraphers came to reject *tiexue* (the study of classic models of calligraphy) as degenerate, and sought aesthetic renewal by way of a return to earlier traditions. Clerical script therefore experienced a revival which was still current during Zheng Xiaoxu's time. For many years, Zheng tried out different techniques and started to develop his own personal genre. As one can see in the next entry, his assiduous copying of early stele models produced a very distinctive style in the late Qing and early Republican era.

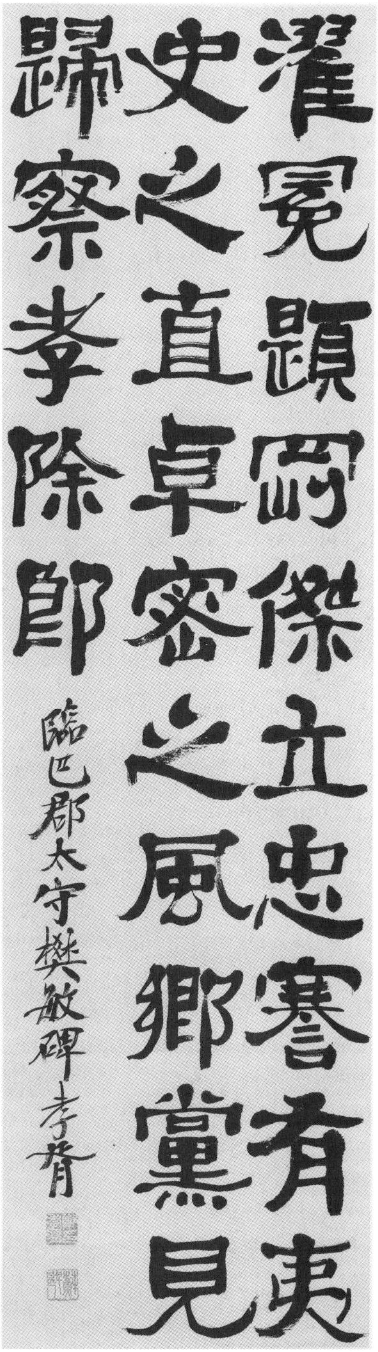

28 ZHENG Xiaoxu 鄭孝胥 (1860–1938)

Two poems in running script 行書詩二首

hanging scroll; ink on paper, 64.5 x 33.5 cm 300.2003

安吳論書家，欲下石如拜。鄧書殊非雅，悪札豈可耐。石庵號蘊藉，堆墨作狡獪。未若何道周，斫陣不挂鎧。何筆晚苦驕，嵬騃近俗態。出林喻飛鳥，我意在無礙。題劉文清行書卷子。

當年晦若嘗相語，絕頂初晴看雪山。煩把峨眉從頭說，不須疾首到時艱。贈趙堯生。

款識：勳閣仁兄大雅正。孝胥。

鈐印：海藏樓。

When Anwu made comments about calligraphers,
He paid high homage to [Deng] *Shiru.*
Deng's calligraphy is not especially inelegant,
Yet some characters in his badly written letters are unbearable.
Shian is known as being connotative and restrained,
Heaping up inks, his works are overly artful and cunning.
They are not at all a match for He Daozhou,
Who never wore armour to enter a battle.
Even he, his late brushes too wilful and impetuous,
Too devious and strange, they merely mean to satisfy vulgar tastes.
Like a bird flying out from a tree grove,
I am suggesting an unrestrained and spontaneous manner.
(Inscribed on a hanging scroll in running script by Liu Wenqing.)
In those damp and gloomy days we once decided,
To climb up the peak and behold the snowy mountains on a clear day.
Please let's talk of Mount E'mei again, from the beginning,
Don't forget it just because there are times of troubles and headaches.
(Written for Zhao Yaosheng.)

Inscription and signature: For the appraisal of Xunge. Xiaoxu.

The first poem in this work is rather interesting because it expresses the author's own view on calligraphy. Anwu is the style name of Bao Shichen (1775–1855), a theorist of calligraphy who was regarded as the prime advocate of the *beixue* (stele school) of calligraphy. Deng Shiru (1743–1805), teacher of Bao Shichen, was also recognised as a leading figure in the *beixue* movement during the mid Qing period. His style of innovative seal and clerical scripts proved highly influential for many later prominent *beixue* calligraphers. Shian is the alias of Liu Yong (1719–1804), a renowned scholar-official, who was regarded as one of the four most respected calligraphers of the

Qianlong and Jiajing reigns. In his calligraphy he dramatically varies the pressure of his brush; because of his heavy, thick brushstrokes his calligraphy was at times sneered at as being *mozhu* 墨豬 or 'pigink' (suggesting it had features that were 'fat'). He Daozhou refers to He Shaoji (1799–1863), a distinguished calligrapher of the mid Qing dynasty, whose later works, written in regular and cursive scripts, look like works of abstract art, giving each character a remarkable and unexpected shape. Among all of them, except for Liu Yong who was a calligrapher following the *tiexue* tradition, the rest were associated with the *beixue* movement.

Unlike other influential calligraphers who chose either *beixue* or *tiexue*, Zheng advocated adopting both traditions. His integration of running script based on the Northern Song calligraphers Su Shi and Huang Tingjian, along with the clerical script of early stele models, produced a very distinctive style in the early Republic.

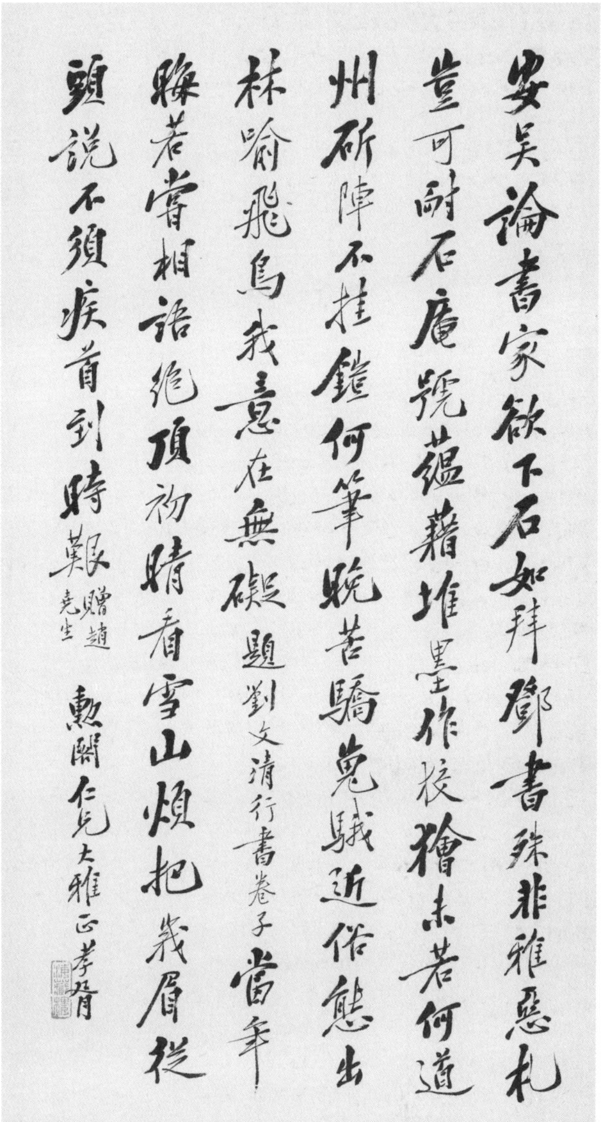

29 DUANFANG 端方 (1861–1911)

Li Bai's poem in semi-cursive script 行書李白《望廬山瀑布》 1905

hanging scroll; ink on paper, 66.3 x 27.1 cm 255.2003

飛流直下三千尺，疑是銀河落九天。
款識：乙巳四月。端方。
鈐印：端方印信。

Vaulting down for three thousand feet,
It's like the Milky Way tumbling from the Nine Heavens.

Inscription and signature: [Written] in the fourth moon of the year *yisi* [1905]. Duanfang.

The ancestors of Duanfang (alias Wu Qiao 午橋, style name Taozhai 匋齋) were originally Han Chinese. They moved from their native place in Zhejiang to Manchuria in the late Ming dynasty, and eventually became Manchu subjects, adopting the clan name Tohoro. Duanfang became an honorary licentiate late in his teens, and served for a few years as a second-class secretary and then as an assistant director of a department in the Board of Works. After he received the *juren* degree in 1882, he obtained many high government appointments, including governor of Hubei province, acting governor-general of Hu-guang (Hunan and Guangdong) and of Liangjiang (in present-day Jiangsu, Anhui and Jiangxi provinces). A modernising high-ranking official of the Qing dynasty, Duanfang was one of five special commissioners who travelled to Western countries to observe the forms of government in 1906. He was a successful official, as well as a renowned collector-connoisseur. In his spare time, he dedicated himself to collecting and studying Chinese antiquities, and assembled a great private collection and published several important catalogues. As Tomas Lawton puts it, 'Almost every museum in the world with a Chinese collection contains some artefacts that have passed through Tuan-fang's hands'.[1]

The lyrical content was drawn from the last two lines of a poem by the great Tang dynasty poet Li Bai (701–762AD), 'Gazing at the waterfall at Mount Lu'. The first two lines read: 'Sunlight flows on the Incense-Burner Peak, sparking a purple haze, / From far to sea, the river hangs high on the cliff'. Duanfang's brushwork reflects the elegant and graceful manner of *tiexue* style: it is decidedly fluent without a trace of hesitation. The overall demeanour conveys a pleasing ease.

1 Tomas Lawton, *A time of transition: two collectors of Chinese art*, Spencer Museum of Art, The University of Kansas 1991, pp 5–64; For Duanfang's life, see also *Qing shigao*, *Biography*, 256

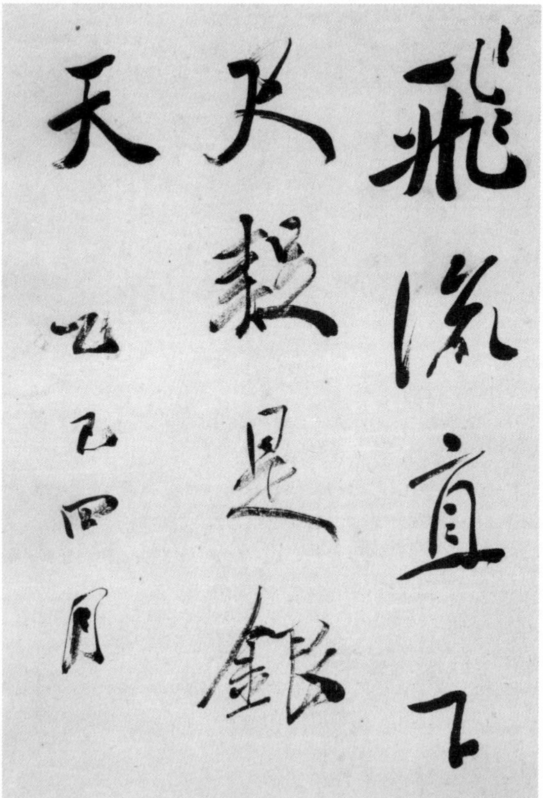
飛流直下三千
尺疑是銀河落九
天
乙巳四月
端方

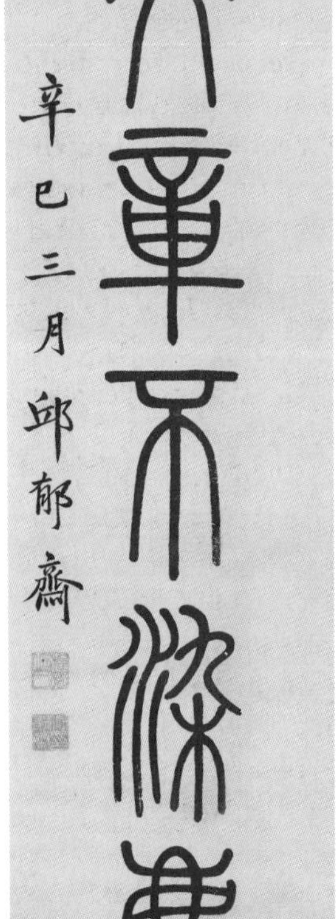
辛巳三月邱郁喬

30 QIU Yuzhai 丘鬱齋 (active c1881)

Couplet in seal script (named side only) 篆書七言聯（缺上聯） c1881

hanging scroll; ink on paper, 134.3 x 26.6 cm 307.2003

秋水文章不染塵。
款識：辛巳三月丘鬱齋。
鈐印：程鄉丘氏。丘郁齋印。

The writing that resembles an autumnal river is never contaminated by dust.

Inscription and signature: In the third moon of the year *xinsi* [1881].

The couplet survives only in the *xialian* (lower piece) that bears the author's name. However, its s*hanglian* (upper piece) can be reconstructed in the light of the same couplet seen elsewhere – the poem of 'the autumnal river-like writings' was always coupled with the following line: 'The spring breeze of great elegance tolerates the myriad things 春風大雅能容物'. The inscription dates the couplet to the year of *xinsi*, which opens to the possible years of 1881 or 1941. On grounds of script style and the materials, 1881 is plausible. As discussed elsewhere, an enthralment with calligraphy on inscriptions recovered from stone stele and bronzes of ancient times was prevalent during the second part of the Qing dynasty. *Zhuanshu* (seal script), the archaic form of writing, experienced a revival and was employed widely in the art of calligraphy, as demonstrated in this couplet. Here, each of the slender and rounded lines is evenly and precisely brushed with well-hidden brush tips, resulting in an iron wire-like feature. Note that the author used *zhongfeng* (the tip of the brush in the centre) all the time; thus the corners are all rounded off. The style, called *yuzhu zhuan* 玉箸篆 (jade chopstick-like seal script), is typical of Li Yangbing's writing (mid 8th century). The Tang dynasty calligrapher was acclaimed the only great master in this script after Li Si of the Qin dynasty.

Except for the date of the couplet, we know virtually nothing about Qiu Yuzhai.

31 **GUI Dian** 桂坫 (1865–1958)

Couplet in regular script (named side only) 楷書八言聯（缺上聯） 1931

hanging scroll; ink on paper, 169 x 35.5 cm 292.2003

盧陵蓄道德能文章。
款識：辛未桂坫。
鈐印：桂坫南屏。莫躓於山而躓於垤。

Luling cherished great morals, and was also an accomplished writer.

Inscription and signature: Written by Gui Dian in the year of *xinwei* [1931].

Luling is the hometown and sobriquet of Wen Tianxiang (1236–83), the famous loyalist minister of the Southern Song dynasty who led a losing war defending it against the invading Mongols. He was to die a martyr after years in captivity, primarily being remembered in China as a patriot and a great poet. The expression 'cherished great morals, and was also an accomplished writer' applied here to Wen is taken from an article written by Zeng Gong (1019–83), one of the eight most famous writers of the Tang and Song dynasties.[1] Zeng criticised the then current practice of epitaph writing with exaggerated praise unworthy of the recipient. He considered that only those who 'cherished great morals', and were 'accomplished writers' deserved an epitaph.

Gui Dian (alias Nanping 南屏), a native of Nanhai, Guangdong, was born into a family of scholar-officials. His father was a prolific Confucian scholar with more than 30 publications to his credit. Gui Dian himself passed the metropolitan examinations to receive his *jinshi* degree in 1894 at the age of 30, and held positions such as prefect of Yanzhou in Zhejiang, and historiographer at the State Historiographer's Office. Ending his official career with the fall of the Qing dynasty, he fled to Hong Kong and supported himself and his family by selling calligraphic works and paintings. Beside his accomplishments in calligraphy, his contribution to scholarship included editing four gazetteers of Guangdong county.

The style of the writing is close to that of the Tang calligrapher Yan Zhenqing and his follower Liu Gongquan (778–865): both emphasised strength, boldness and grandness. Yet in comparison with the style of Yan-Liu, Gui's script tends to be more charming than dynamic.

1 Zeng Gong, 'Ji Ouyang sheren shu 寄歐陽舍人書 (*A letter to Ouyang Xiu*)'

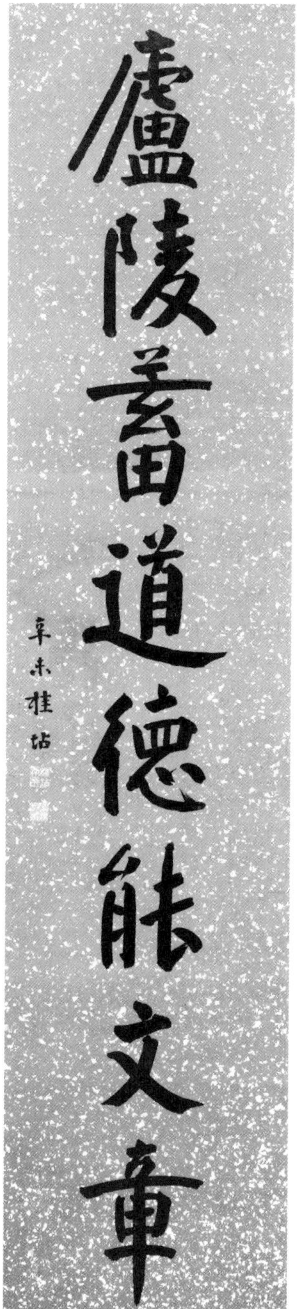
廬陵蓄道德能文章
辛未桂站

32 **GUI Dian** 桂坫 (1865–1958)

'Revisiting Little Ten-thousand-willow Hall' in running script 行書七律《重過小萬柳堂》 1938

hanging scroll; ink on paper, 34.3 x 96.5 cm 247.2005

三度來遊萬柳堂，看書未了看山忙。午晴花韻迴廊靜，秋老桐陰透屋涼。湖面無塵孤夢冷，樓頭有笛一聲長。裁牋我久輟吟詠，媿負詩人廉夕陽。
款識：惠卿有'夕陽穿樹補花紅'之句，人呼爲'廉夕陽'。重過小萬柳堂，柳珍女士采覽。戊寅夏桂坫書與九龍。
鈐印：桂坫長壽。翰林散館夷三。儒林後人。

For the third time I came to visit Ten-thousand-willow Hall,
Reading books shall never pass, but now I am fully occupied gazing at mountains.
The fine afternoon scent of flowers lingers around the quiet veranda,
In the shade of wutong trees the autum is wearing on, and the entire house is cool.
Wandering above the dustless lake my dream alone feels chilly,
On top of the pavilion a flute echoes from far away.
While preparing the paper I realise I have stopped writing for some time,
I feel ashamed when I recite Lian's wonderful line 'the setting sun'.

Inscription and signature: [Lian] Huiqing once wrote the famous line, 'The setting sun through tree grove replenishes the red of blossoms', which won him the name of 'Setting-sun Lian'. Revisting the Little Ten-thousand-willow Hall, written for Ms Liu Zhen by Gui Dian at Kowloon [in Hong Kong] in the summer of the year *wuyin* [1938].

The Little Ten-thousand-willow Hall, located at the West Lake in Hangzhou, was built originally during Guangxu's reign (r1875–1908) as a retreat by Lian Huiqing, a famous painter, seal carver, poet and collector in Wuxi, Jiangsu province. During the Xuantong period (1909–11) a rich businessman, Jiang Guobang, bought and expanded it; thereafter its name was changed to Jiangzhuang, and it remains one of best preserved private gardens in Hangzhou today.

This poem conveys a melancholy feeling which is embodied in the serene scenery: autumn is wearing on, the soul withers. The poet seems to express a spiritual helplessness with a sigh: he has let time slip by without accomplishing anything. Tension is created between the conflicting images of enduring nature and an idle old man. The work reflects another feature of Gui Dian's calligraphic style, which quite suits the sentiment expressed. Here, the spaciousness and breadth of the Yan-Liu style seen in the couplet of the previous entry have disappeared: the script is rather slim, pretty, feminine and loose, rather than upright, muscular and controlled.

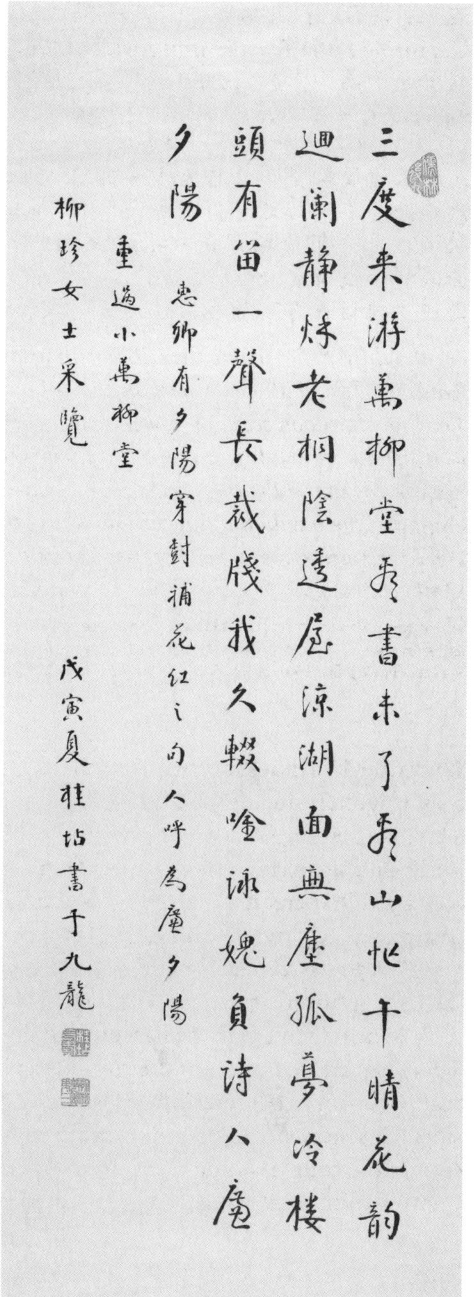
三度来游萬柳堂夏書未了夏山忙千晴花韵
迴闌静炼老桐陰透屋凉湖面無塵孤夢冷楼
頭有笛一聲長裁牋我久輟唫詠媿負詩人屬
夕陽
惠卿有夕陽穿封補花红之句人呼為屬夕陽
重過小萬柳堂
柳珍女士采覽
戊寅夏桂坫書于九龍

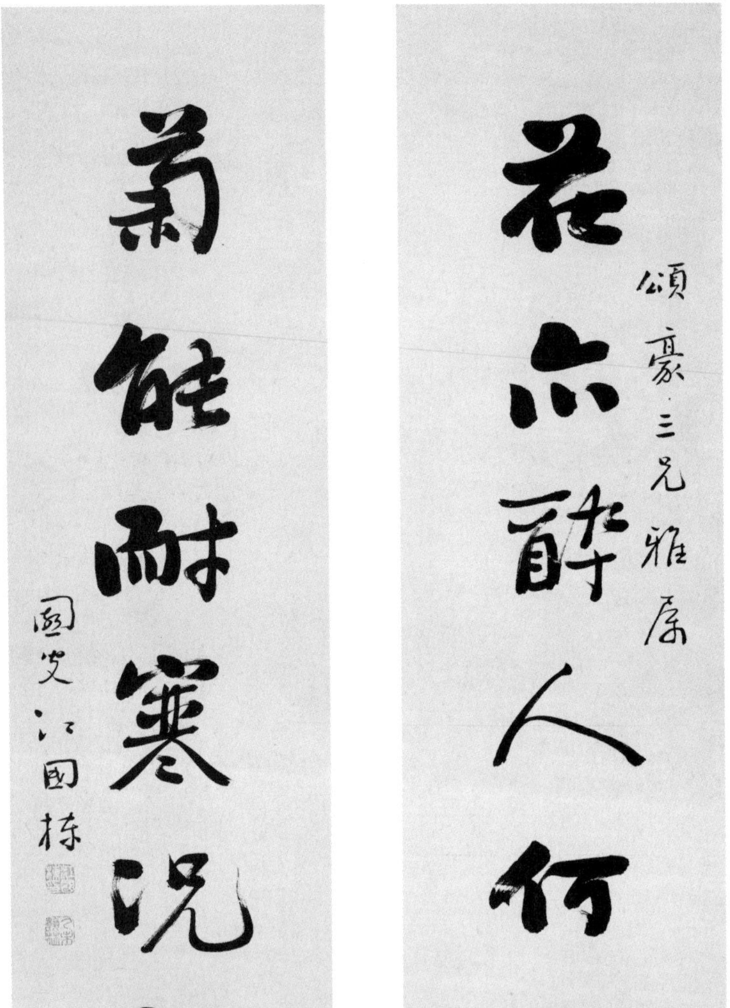
花亦醉人何必酒
頌豪三兄雅屬
菊能耐寒況於松
國文 江國棟

33 **JIANG Guodong** 江國棟 (*jinshi* 1895)

Couplet in running script 行書七言聯

pair of hanging scrolls; ink on paper, 41.2 x 169.5 cm each 303.2003.a-b

花亦醉人何必酒；菊能耐寒況於松。
款識：園叟江國棟。
鈐印：江國棟印。乙未翰林。

When flowers can intoxicate, why desire wine?
Just like the pine tree, the chrysanthemum also endures the cold.

Inscription and signature: Jiang Guodong, alias Yuansou.

Jiang Guodong (style name Yuansou 園叟, also known as Yunchen 蘊琛) was a native of Rongxian in Guangxi province. He gained the *jinshi* degree in the year of *yiwei* (1895) which made him very proud, as he carved this piece of information in a seal, which can be seen in this work. He served in various low-ranking posts such as magistrate of Lijiang prefecture in Yunnan. After the fall of the Qing dynasty in 1911 he travelled, wandering throughout the Malay Archipelago; he also went to Taiwan several times.

Jiang was known as a poet and calligrapher and had published an anthology of his own poems entitled *Dongning chouchang ji* 東寧酬唱集. He excelled in regular and running scripts, of which this work is an example. It appears that his writing absorbed the horizontal emphasis of the clerical script to create the unique and bold style seen in this work.

34 **LI Zhanzhi** 黎湛枝 (c1870–1929)

Couplet in running script 行書八言聯

pair of hanging scrolls; ink on paper, 43.1 x 186.5 cm each 285.2003.a-b

古今畢陳趣生一室；人天興感文可萬言。
款識：露苑黎湛枝。
鈐印：臣黎湛枝。露苑。

The present and the past come together, the room is filled with joy;
When men commune with the Heavens, even a small piece of writing can attain ten thousand words.

Inscription and signature: Li Zhanzhi, alias Luyuan.

The couplet describes joy of the scholar on his cultured life in solitary study. Within this studio – his room for study and contemplation – he surrounded himself with cultural implements, and also evoked a sense of spiritual vitality, where the present encounters the past and the individual communes with the universe. With a blend of history and transcendence, the private, insular life implied in a study is somehow dignified.

Li Zhanzhi (alias Luyuan 露苑) was one of many poor scholars to succeed in their ambitions through the civil service examination. Born into an ordinary family at Lidong village in Foshan, Guangdong, he received his *jinshi* degree in 1903, and was the *chuanlu* (first in the second class). He became a member of the Hanlin Academy, was awarded the title of the Grand Guardian of the Heir Apparent, and served as one of the tutors of the last emperor Puyi (r1909–11). The couplet, suggesting in a general way the demeanour of Dong Qichang and Zhao Mengfu's writing, is a good example of the enduring quality of *tiexue* tradition at the Qing court.

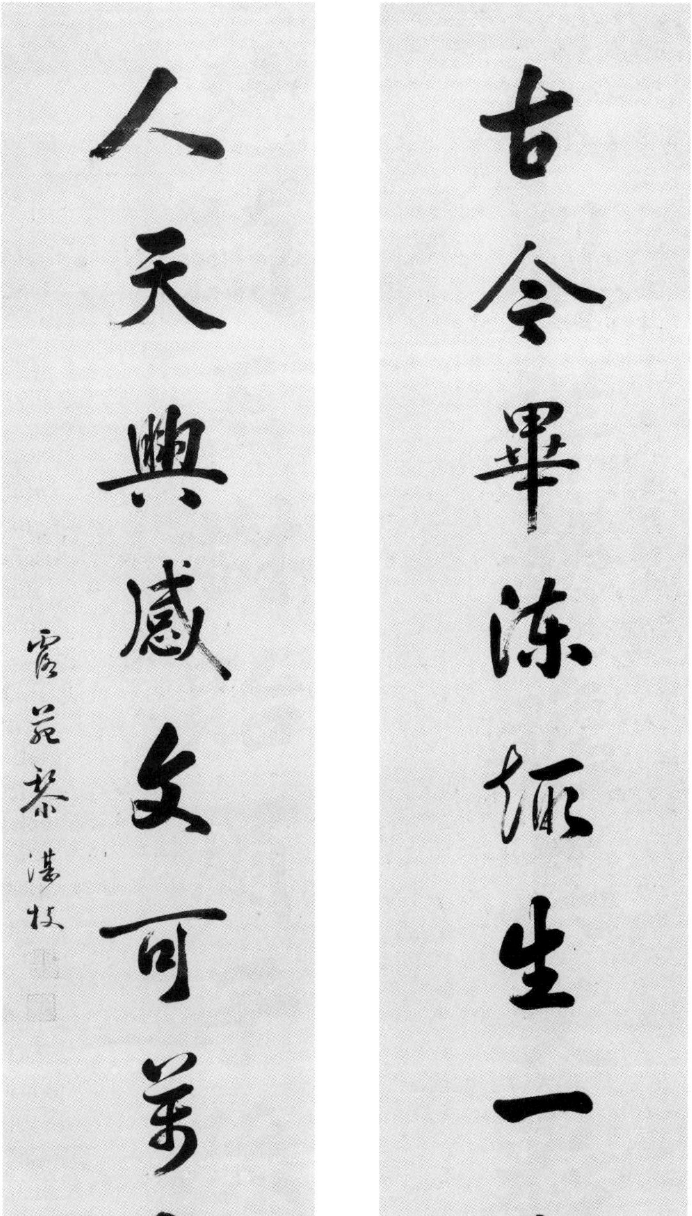
古今畢陳纙生一宝
人天興感文可萬言

35 ZHU Ruzhen 朱汝珍 (1869–1942)

Wang Wan's poem in running script 行書汪琬七絕《過石塢》

hanging scroll; ink on paper, 125 x 40.9 cm 293.2003

主賓無語似相忘，淨掃青苔坐夕陽。乳燕飛飛蛙閣閣，楚萍謝絮滿池塘。
款識：汪鈍翁過石塢一首。宗魯仁兄雅屬。隘園朱汝珍。
鈐印：朱汝珍字聘三。甲辰榜眼。

Cleaning up lichen and sitting under the setting sun,
Both host and guest are silent, as if keeping themselves aloof from the world.
Young swallows flutter in the air, frogs croak below;
Duckweed and willow catkins fill the pool.

Inscription and signature: Transcription of 'Passing by Shiwu', a poem by Wang Dunweng [1624–1691]. Written for Zonglu as he requested. Zhu Ruzhen, style name Aiyuan.

The poem, composed by Wang Wan (1624–1691, style name Dunweng), a scholar-official and well-known poet of Emperor Kangxi's court, expresses a serene communion between humanity and nature that stimulates in one's mind an awakening, a purge, and a sublime transcendence of mortal bounds.

Zhu Ruzhen (alias Pinsan 聘三, style name Aiyuan 隘園) was a native of Qingyuan, Guangdong province. Born into a poor family (his father died when he was young), he passed the metropolitan examination in 1904, a year before the imperial examination system was abolished, and gained his *jinshi* degree, taking second place (*bangyan* 榜眼) which he indicates in one of his seals. As a compiler of the Hanlin Academy, he was chosen to study law in Japan in 1905. Upon his graduation and return to China, he became a professor at the Law School in Beijing. He resettled in Hong Kong after China became a republic, and taught at Hong Kong University.

Although during Zhu's time, the calligraphic style based on the Northern Wei stele was predominant, he seemed to have been able to immerse himself in the style of the *tiexue* tradition. In his early life, Zhu Ruzhen followed the style of Zhao Mengfu, and his elegantly balanced *kaishu* script was admired by Puyi, the last Qing emperor – even in the early republic Puyi still requested Zhu write pieces which were to be bestowed on his formal courtiers.[1] His running script seeks only a slight change within a restrictive scheme. Many scholar-officials had, since childhood, studied the *guan'geti* 館閣體 (a style based on regular script but well-knit, required for the imperial civil service examination) and thus found it difficult to significantly depart from the style; Zhu Ruzhen's calligraphy is a good example.

1 See Lin Yajie and Zhu Wanzhang (eds), p 115, fig 12

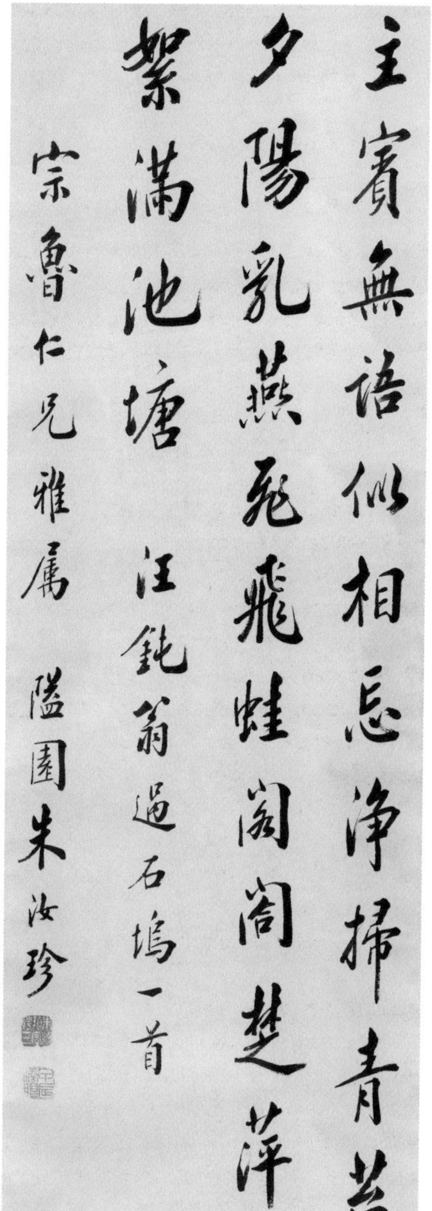
主賓無語似相忘淨掃青苔坐
夕陽乳燕飛飛蛙閣閣楚萍謝
絮滿池塘
汪鈍翁過石塢一首
宗魯仁兄雅屬
隘園朱汝珍

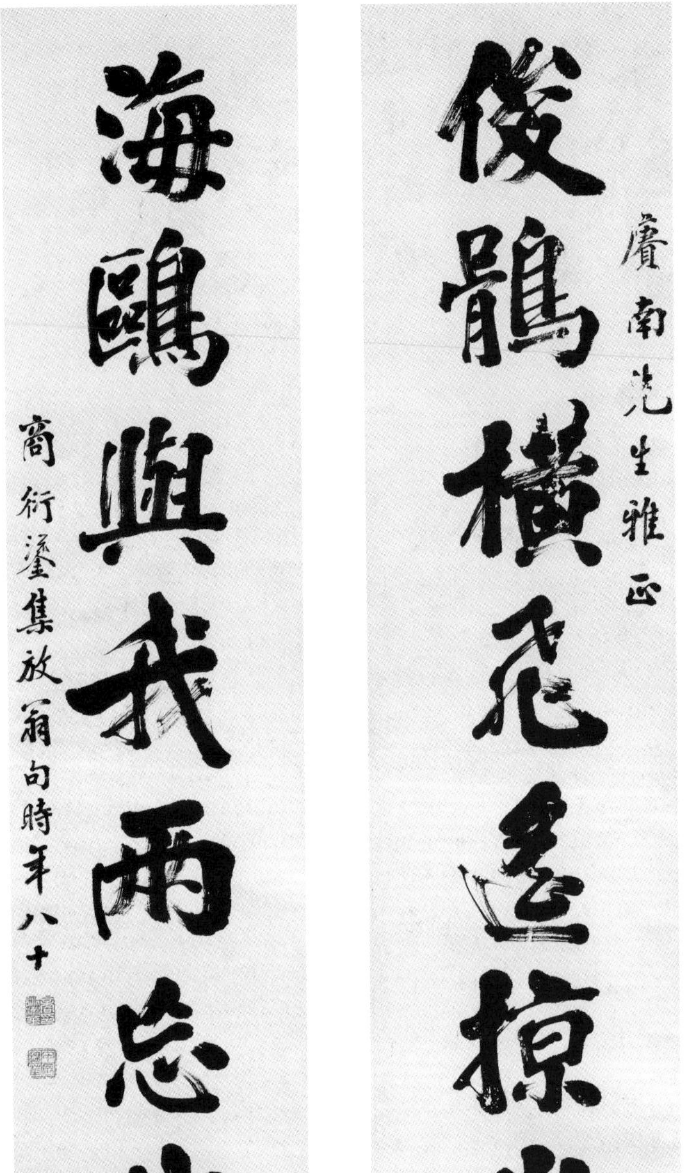
俊鶻橫飛遙掠岸
賡南先生雅正
海鷗與我兩忘機
商衍鎏集放翁句時年八十

36 SHANG Yanliu 商衍鎏 (1875–1963)

Couplet of Lu You's poem in semi-cursive script 行草集陸遊詩七言聯 c1955

pair of hanging scrolls; ink on paper, 135.5 x 31.2 cm each

俊鶻橫飛遙掠岸，海鷗與我兩忘機。
款識：賡南先生雅正。商衍鎏集放翁句時年八十。
鈐印：商衍鎏印。甲辰探花。

In the distance, a robust falcon skirts the coast swiftly;
Holding our minds aloof from the world, there is only me and the seagulls.

Inscription and signature: For the appraisal of Mr Geng'nan. Assembling poems by Lu You, written by Shang Yanliu at the age of 80.

Shang Yanliu (alias Zaoting 藻亭, style name Youzhang 又章) was a native of Panyu (present-day Guangzhou). He earned the coveted *jinshi* degree in 1904, taking the third place (he carved this piece of information in the second seal on this couplet), and became a member of the Hanlin Academy. In 1906, he was sent to Japan along with Zhu Ruzhen to study law and constitution matters. He remained there until 1909. Between 1909 and 1912 he was a professor of Chinese at the Overseas Commercial College in Hamburg. Upon returning to Beijing, he served in the Republican government as an adviser to the vice-president, then to the president, and was a special delegate for the Finance Department to Jiangxi. After 1949, he served for some years as the deputy director of the Central Research Institute of History Archive. He is considered a scholar and calligrapher, and his most well-known book was *Accounts of the imperial civil service examination in the Qing dynasty* 清代科舉考試述錄. His calligraphy is highly treasured, especially when it is grouped along with works by Liu Chunlin, Zhu Ruzhen and Zhang Qihou who took first place (*zhuangyuan*), second place (*bangyan*) and the fourth place (*chuanlu*) respectively, in the highest level of the last imperial civil service examination – the group called *jidi siping* 及第四屏.

The couplet is composed of lines taken from two separate poems by Lu You of the Southern Song dynasty.[1] It expresses a typical Chinese literati's view of phenomena: by communicating with the natural realm, one can escape the disturbing pressures of the mundane world. The brushwork in this couplet is bold and vigorous, which reflects the influence of the Tang calligrapher Yan Zhengqing. The broad brush tip sweeps over the paper, leaving traces of white which contrast with the strokes in heavy ink, providing a source of calligraphic charm.

1 Su Shi, 'Departure from Yiling 初發夷陵', and 'Sitting alone 獨坐'

37 **ZHANG Qihou** 張啓後 (? – after 1940)

Poem by Lu You in running script 行書陸游七絕《看鏡》

hanging scroll; ink on paper, 49.7 x 203 cm 295.2003

凋盡朱顏白盡頭，神仙富貴兩悠悠。胡塵遮斷陽關路，空聽琵琶奏石州。
款識：放翁詩。張啓後。
鈐印：張啓後印。甲辰傳臚。

The rosy cheek is faded, and the hair has turned grey,
Immortality and wealth remain a remote dream.
Mounted Tartars have blocked the Yang Pass with dust,
One just helplessly listens to a pipa lute lamenting on Shizhou.

Inscription and signature: A poem by Fangweng [Lu You]. Zhang Qihou.

Two years before Lu You was born, the Jurchens (a Tungus ethnic group inhabiting parts of Manchuria) overran most of North China in 1126 and established the Jin dynasty. The Song court retreated to the south to re-establish the Southern Song in present-day Hangzhou. Throughout his life, Lu You held a patriotic stance, advocating the expulsion of the Jurchen from northern China. This was the cause of his pain and source of his poetic inspiration. The poem was written when he was between 60 and 70 years old, during two decades of retirement at his birthplace, Shaoxing. Entitled *Gazing into a mirror*, it is a lament on the delusions of this life and the division of his country (Shizhou is a city in the north).

Zhang Qihou (alias Yanchang 燕昌, style name Ruoceng 若曾), a native of Sizhou in Anhui, was the *chuanlu* (first in the second class) of *jinshi* in the last imperial civil service examination of 1904. Since there were only three recipients of the degree in the first class, *chuanlu* naturally assumed the fourth on the list. When grouped with the work of the other three *jinshi* degree holders, his calligraphy is in high demand. Zhang's last years were spent in retirement in Shanghai, supporting himself by selling calligraphy and writing articles. In this work, he used a very absorbent paper and a brush well loaded with ink, thus revealing the subtleties of ink density on the absorbent surface of paper.

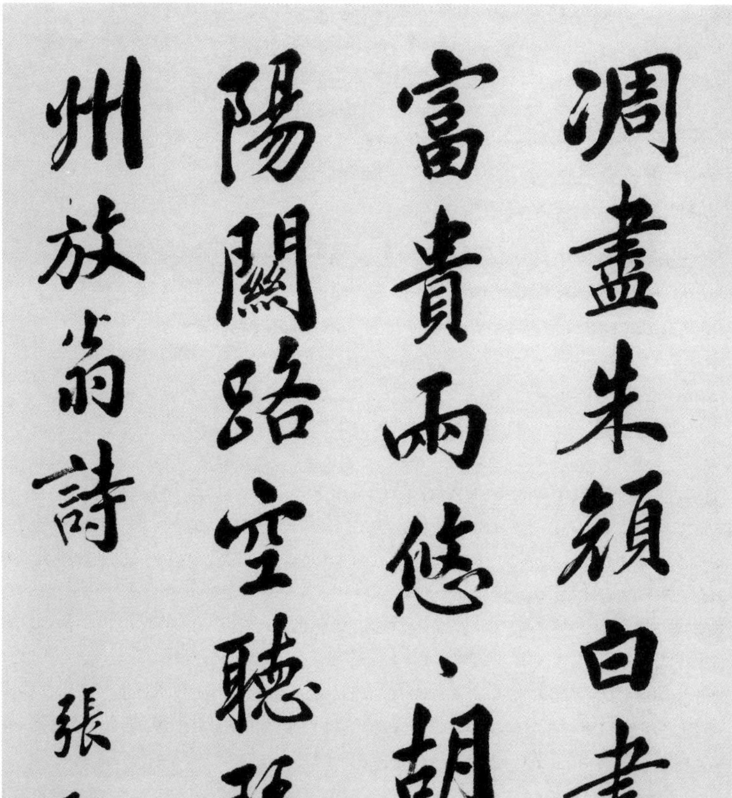
凋盡朱顏白盡頭神仙
富貴兩悠悠胡塵遮斷
陽關路空聽琵琶奏石
州放翁詩
張啓後

38 **OU Dayuan** 區大原 (after 1877 – ?)

Couplet in regular script 楷書七言聯

pair of hanging scrolls; ink on paper, 32 x 132.4 cm each 284.2003.a-b

鐵硯磨穿爲俊傑；福田收穫在後人。
款識：硯田仁兄大雅屬。區大原。
鈐印：區大原印。桂海。

By using up an inkstone one can become a person of outstanding accomplishment;
To plough the fields guarantees a harvest for your descendants.

Insciption and signature: [Written] at the request of Yantian, Ou Dayuan.

The charm and allusion of this couplet depends upon word play and puns which are partly phonetic, partly allusive. It obliquely hints at the recipient's name (Yantian) by highlighting the two images of *yan* (inkstone) and *tian* (rice field). The poetic expression and meaning are cunningly composed around these two characters. 'Using up an inkstone' alludes to the years traditional Chinese scholars spend studying the ancient classics and philosophical treatises in the hope of passing the civil service examination. Passing this examination allowed them to enter government service, the key to a life of privilege that would benefit their descendants.

The couplet would be encouraging for an enterprising scholar, while also mirroring the author's own experience. Ou Dayuan grew up in an ordinary family in a village called Songtang in Nanhai, Guangdong. In 1903, along with his cousin Ou Dadian, he qualified in the metropolitan examination and was granted the *jinshi* degree. His career as a bachelor at the Hanlin Academy did not last long. The two cousins fled to Hong Kong when the Qing dynasty fell. Ou Dayuan spent the rest of his life there, supporting himself mainly by selling his calligraphy.

The couplet was composed in *kaishu* (regular script). During the Qing period, *kaishu* was a must for all novices of calligraphy and a stepping stone to official success. The system of civil service examinations not only placed a premium on the good command of calligraphy, but also developed a writing style, known as *guan'geti* (script of cabinet), derived from regular script, but stiffer, almost like printed text. Its required features were that it be black, square, smooth and even. All candidates of the examination consciously adopted this style of calligraphy. This couplet reflects such a style.

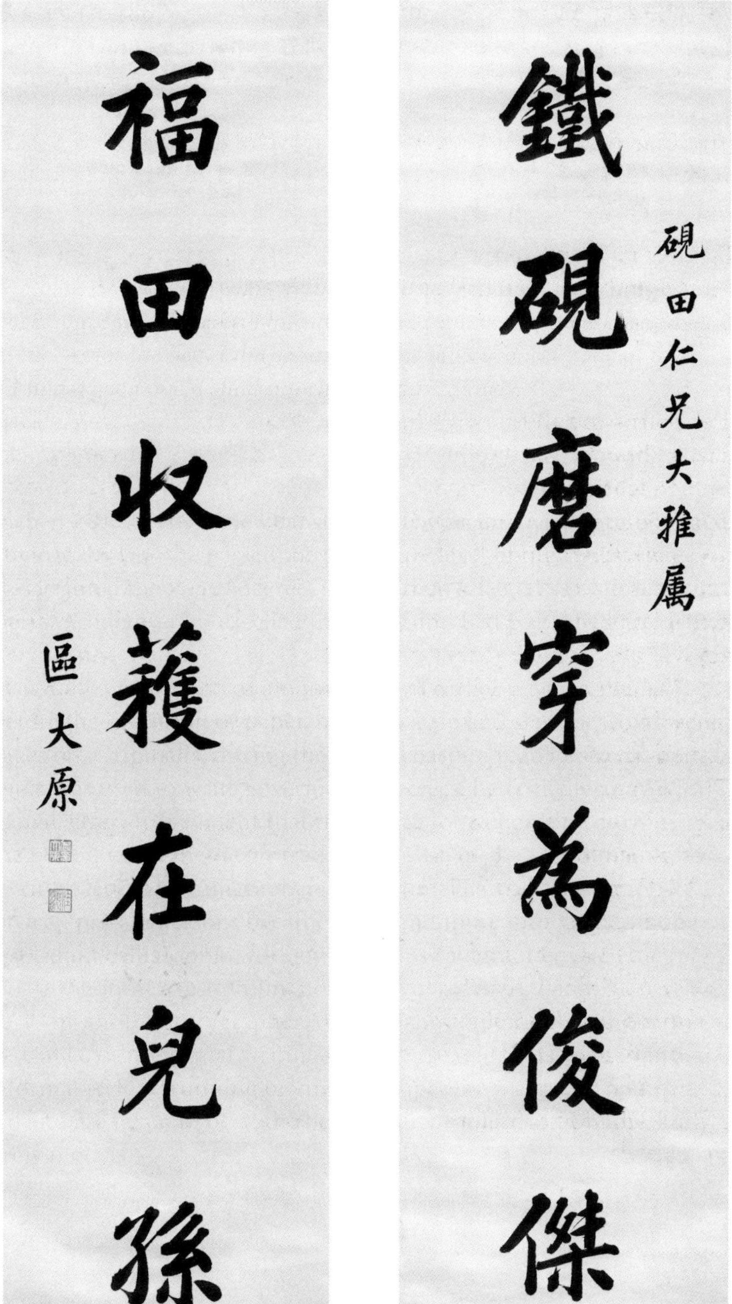
鐵硯磨穿為俊傑
硯田仁兄大雅屬
福田收穫在兒孫
區大原

39 **FENG Baili** 馮百勵 (1878–1960)

Couplet in cursive script 草書七言聯 1947

pair of hanging scrolls; ink on paper, 39.8 x 154.5 each 297.2003.a-b

今既見心即見佛，子安知我不知魚。
款識：丁亥秋馮百勵。
鈐印：百勵。

As soon as you catch sight of your mind, you behold the Buddhahood;
How do you know if I know about fish pleasure or not?

Inscription and signature: Feng Baili in the autumn of the year of *dinghai* [1947].

The first line of the couplet refers to the Mahayana Buddhist idea that every ordinary being can reach enlightenment and become Buddha. A foolish passing thought makes one an ordinary man, while an enlightened second thought that frees one from attachments makes one a Buddha. The second line of the couplet alludes to a story recounted in *Zhuangzi* by the 4th century BCE philosopher of the same name. When he and his friend Huizi saw fish swimming placidly near the surface of the water, Zhangzi says: 'That must be their pleasure'. Huizi asked: 'You are not a fish, how do you know if it is their pleasure or not?' Zhuangzi replied: 'You are not me. How do you know if I know about their pleasure or not?' The story implies that it is sometimes possible to notice beautiful things even without reason, or that only those who understand can understand.

Feng Baili (style name Shaobo 少波) was a native of Panyu (in present-day Guangzhou). In his early years, he followed Sun Yat-sen (1866–1925), the Chinese revolutionary, and joined the revolutionary league Tongmenghui. When the Qing dynasty was overthrown and the Chinese republic was established, he served as a presidential adviser in 1918. He was once the chief editor of *Tiansheng Daily*, a newspaper established in 1918 at Guangzhou. He also served as principal of the Sun Yat-sen Memorial School in the same city during 1946–47.

In the hands of many calligraphers, the cursive script was exploited for its expressive, aesthetic potential. Often it was the vehicle in which a calligrapher could express his individuality. The calligraphers' desire to reflect their emotions in their writings is epitomised by this couplet. The abbreviated characters and the carefree disposition of the brushwork are suited perfectly to the ease and calm sentiment they express.

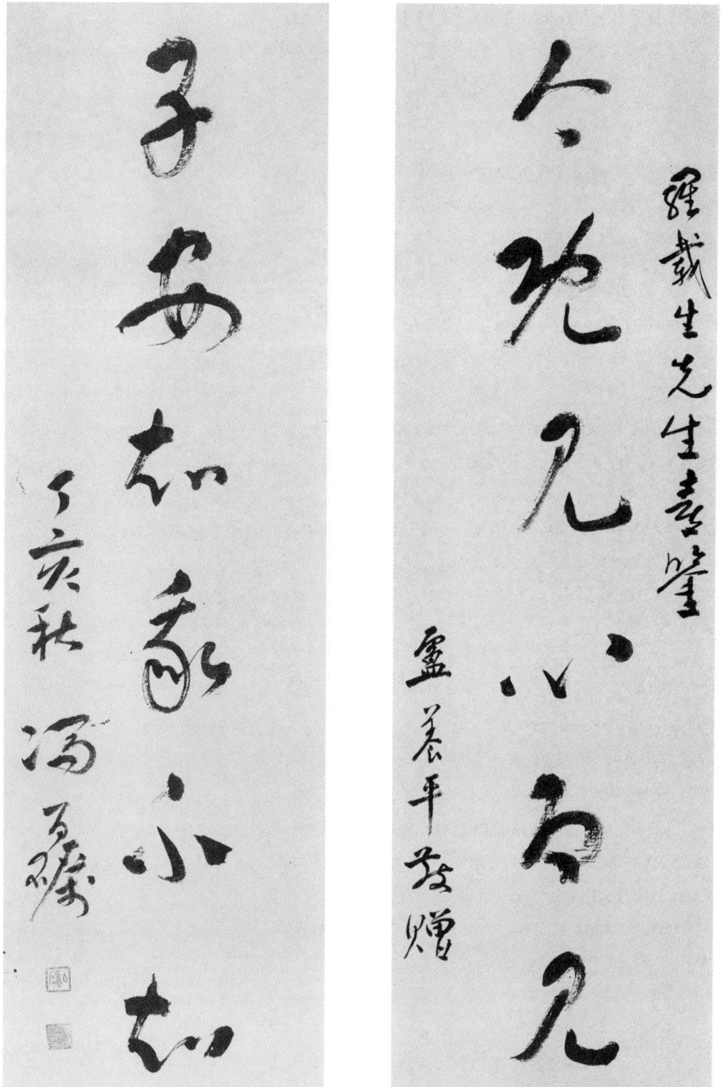

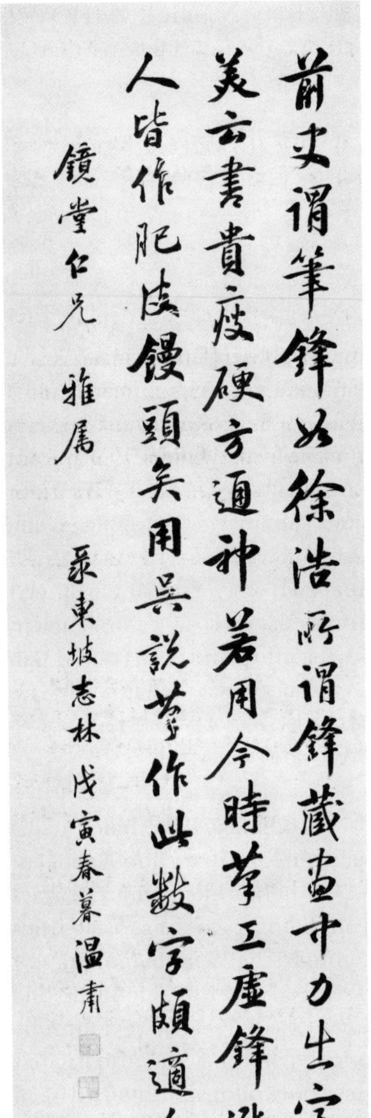
前史謂筆鋒如徐浩所謂鋒藏畫中力出字外杜子
美云書貴瘦硬方通神若用今時筆工虛鋒漲墨則人
人皆作肥皮饅頭矣用吳說筆作此數字頗適人意
鏡堂仁兄雅屬
錄東坡志林 戊寅春暮温肅

40 **WEN Su** 溫肅 (1878–1939)

Su Shi's 'comments on calligraphy' in running script 行書錄《東坡志林》 1938

hanging scroll; ink on paper, 144.5 x 38.4 cm 286.2003

前史謂筆鋒如徐浩，所謂鋒藏畫中，力出字外。杜子美云，書貴瘦硬方通神。若用今時筆工，虛鋒漲墨，則人人皆作肥皮饅頭矣。用吳説筆作此數字，頗適人意。

款識：鏡堂仁兄雅屬。錄東坡志林。戊寅春暮，溫肅。

鈐印：溫肅私印。太史氏。

The previous critics saw the brushstroke of Xu Hao as hiding the tip within the composition, yet the strength well surpassed the limits of the character. Du Zimei [Du Fu 712–770] *says that a piece of calligraphy is valued for its slenderness and toughness since only in this style can characters communicate with the divine. If one follows the current brush method, then the stroke will be done with sapless tips, though loaded fully with ink; and every character will look like a fat steam cake.* [I] *painted this paragraph using Wu Yue's brush style, which is quite satisfactory.*

Inscription and signature: Recording of *Dongpo zhilin* [by Su Shi], brushed at the request of Jingtang, by Wen Su, in late spring of the year *wuyin* [1938].

The passage was taken from *Dongpo zhilin* (Records on the eastern slope) by Su Shi. Xu Hao (703–782) is a renowned calligrapher of the Tang dynasty who carried on the tradition of Wang Xizhi, but had a distinctive style of his own. His calligraphy, the characters plump and vigorous, has the reputation of 'hiding tip' yet 'exuding vigour'. Wu Yue was a renowned calligrapher of the mid 12th century; his small-scale regular script was considered unexcelled during the Song dynasty.

Su comments on the beginnings and ends of brushstrokes and whether the tip of the brush is visible or not while executing a stroke. The expression 'hiding tip' refers to the way the calligrapher makes the brush double back on the initial stroke to conceal the entry point – the spot where brush first meets paper. However if this is overstressed, it may result in what has been ridiculed as 'a fat steam cake': plump strokes with a lack of strength. Xiao Hao is considered a master of control, attaining the level of 'hiding tip'.

Wen Su (alias Yifu 毅夫) was a native of Shunde, Guangdong province. He attained the *jinshi* degree in the year *guimao* (1903). As a member of the Hanlin Academy, he, along with Wang Guowei, was made an adviser to Emperor Guangxu (r1875–1909), carrying out duties at the emperor's Southern Study. He was appointed the censor, and was later sent to Japan to make an on-the-spot investigation of the education system. His graceful running script is a good example of the calligraphy of mandarins of the late Qing, who sought change within a highly regulated and restrictive system.

41 SUN Zhimin 孫智敏 (1881–1961)

Excerpt of Zhang Xuan's epitaph in regular script 楷書《張玄墓誌》 1947

hanging scroll; ink on paper, 76.6 x 21 cm 306.2003

鬱矣蘭胄，茂乎芳幹。葉暎霄衢，根通海翰。休氣貫嶽，榮光接漢。德與風翔，澤從雨散。

款識：強圉大淵獻仲春之月，孫智敏。

鈐印：錢塘孫氏。智敏印信。

A descendant of the orchid, its fragrant branch is luxuriant and exuberant. Its leaves cast light in the sky and thoroughfare, its roots stretch towards the vast sea. Its dauntless spirit penetrates sacred mountains, and its glory connects to the Milky Way. Its virtue soars along with the wind, its lustre scatters with the rain.

Inscription and signature: Written in middle spring of the year *dinghai* [1947] by Sun Zhiming.

Inscriptions carved on stele from the Northern Wei dynasty (386–534) are in the style of regular script. Appearing during the transition era, it was to reflect a bold innovative spirit and an outstanding creative ability in the Tang dynasty (618–907), when the evolution from clerical to regular script occurred. With the decline of the *teixue* tradition (based on classical calligraphic models), stele script became the central focus of a calligraphic revival movement from the mid Qing dynasty until its demise. Among a number of highly praised model stele was the so-called 'Epitaph of Zhang Xuang' (or 'Zhang Heinü' – 'Heinü' was the style name of the deceased), carved in 531. The original stone had long gone missing; however an old ink rubbing of the inscription was rediscovered in the early 19th century by He Shaoji (1799–1863), an advocate of the stele script, who promoted it vigorously. It is a segment of this epitaph that was copied by Sun Zhimin in this hanging scroll.

Sun Zhimin (alias Qincai 廑才), a native of Hangzhou, was awarded the *jinshi* degree in 1903, at the age of 23, and at the same time became a member of the prestigious Hanlin Academy. Soon after, he was sent to Japan to study law. Upon his return to China, he established a law school and a ladies' college in Hangzhou. Between 1910–12, he was the chancellor of Zhejiang College (precursor to Zhejiang University). During his life, he wrote scores of poems and was a well-known calligrapher who generously satisfied anybody who requested his work. His regular script, as demonstrated in this scroll, is formal, dignified but not lacking in elegance, reflecting a typically formal imperial scholar-official's calligraphic style.

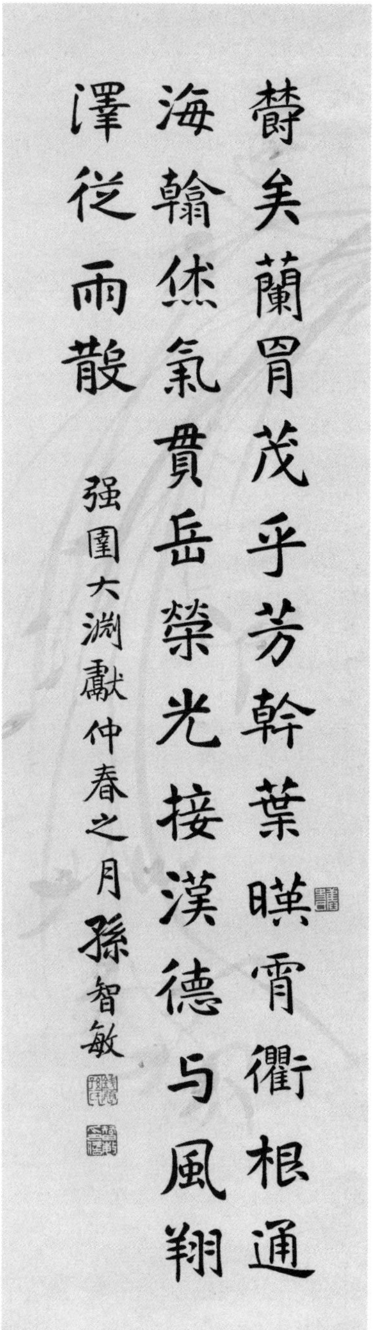
欝矣蘭冐茂乎芳幹葉暎霄衢根通
海翰然氣貫岳榮光接漢德与風翔
澤從雨散
强圉大淵獻仲春之月孫智敏

42 **LI Wenzhao** 李文沼 (? – after 1941)

Couplet in running script 行書七言聯

pair of hanging scrolls; ink on paper, 31 x 152.5 each 308.2003.a-b

花開並蒂鴛鴦暖；酒醉同心琥珀濃。
款識：采蘩李文沼。
鈐印：李文沼印。采蘩印信長壽。

Twin flowering blooms warm a pair of mandarin ducks;
Intertwined hearts are intoxicated, reflected in an amber cup.

Inscription and signature: Li Wenzhao.

It was common practice (and still is in China) to send a couplet to relatives or friends on the occasion of a wedding, as exemplified by these lines. In Chinese literature, twin flowers on one stalk (or pedicel) symbolise a devoted couple. The pair of mandarin ducks is also a customary image of lovers.

Li Wenzhao (alias Caifan 采蘩) was a native of Tianjing. Literary references to him are limited. We only know that he was the follower of Zhang Zhaoxiang (1852–1908), a famous Tianjing painter. Some of his paintings bear the date 1941, suggesting he was still active in the early 1940s.

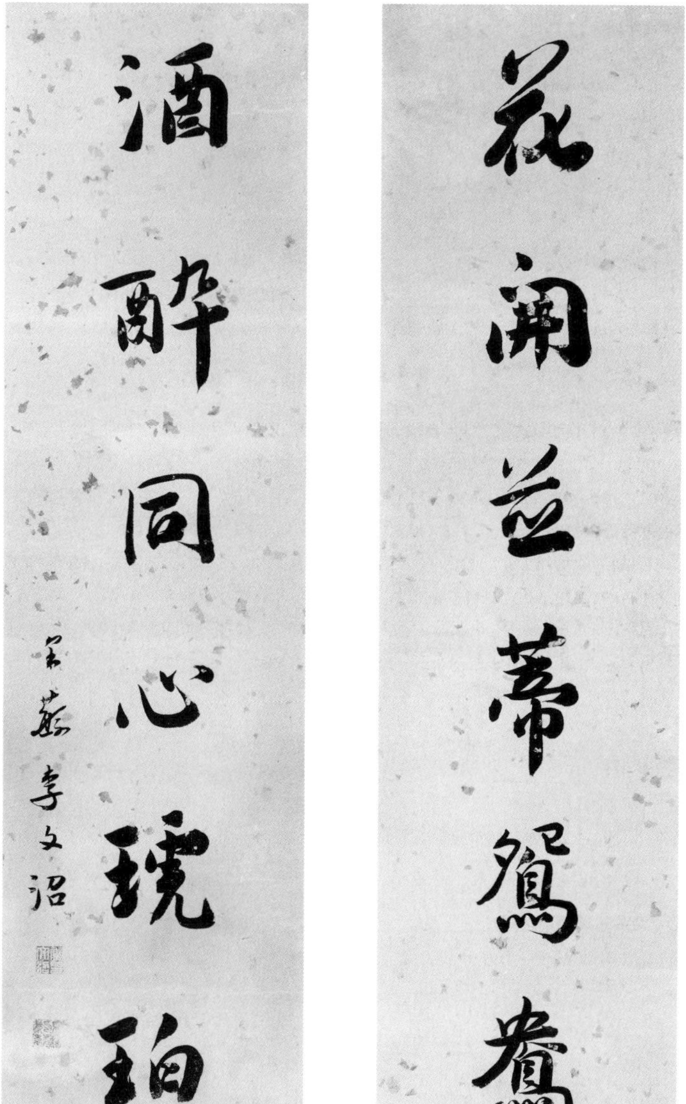
花開並蒂鴛鴦暖
酒醉同心琥珀濃
李文沼

43 **LIANG Song** 梁嵩 (c19th century)

Couplet in cursive script 行書七言聯

pair of hanging scrolls; ink on paper, 37.3 x 144.5 cm each 312.2003.a-b

煙村到處千家暖，猿峽風生兩袖清。
款識：海濤宗兄大人雅屬。西農弟嵩書。
鈐印：梁嵩。操農。

Smoke-veiled village, the warm air shadows thousands of houses;
Monkey-roared gorges, the sleeves are swaying with a gust of wind.

Inscription and signature: For Mr Haitao as he requested, written by Song, alias Xi'nong.

At first glance, the couplet represents a sweet pastoral landscape. The image in the second line, however, may suggest a deeper reading: in Chinese literature 'sleeves swayed with a gust of wind' alludes to the expression of a white-handed official free from corruption and bribery (the long and wide sleeves of a mandarin could serve as the best receptacle to drop money or valuables in). With such an overtone the couplet would be a meaningful motto for an official scholar.

Nothing is known of the life of Liang Song.

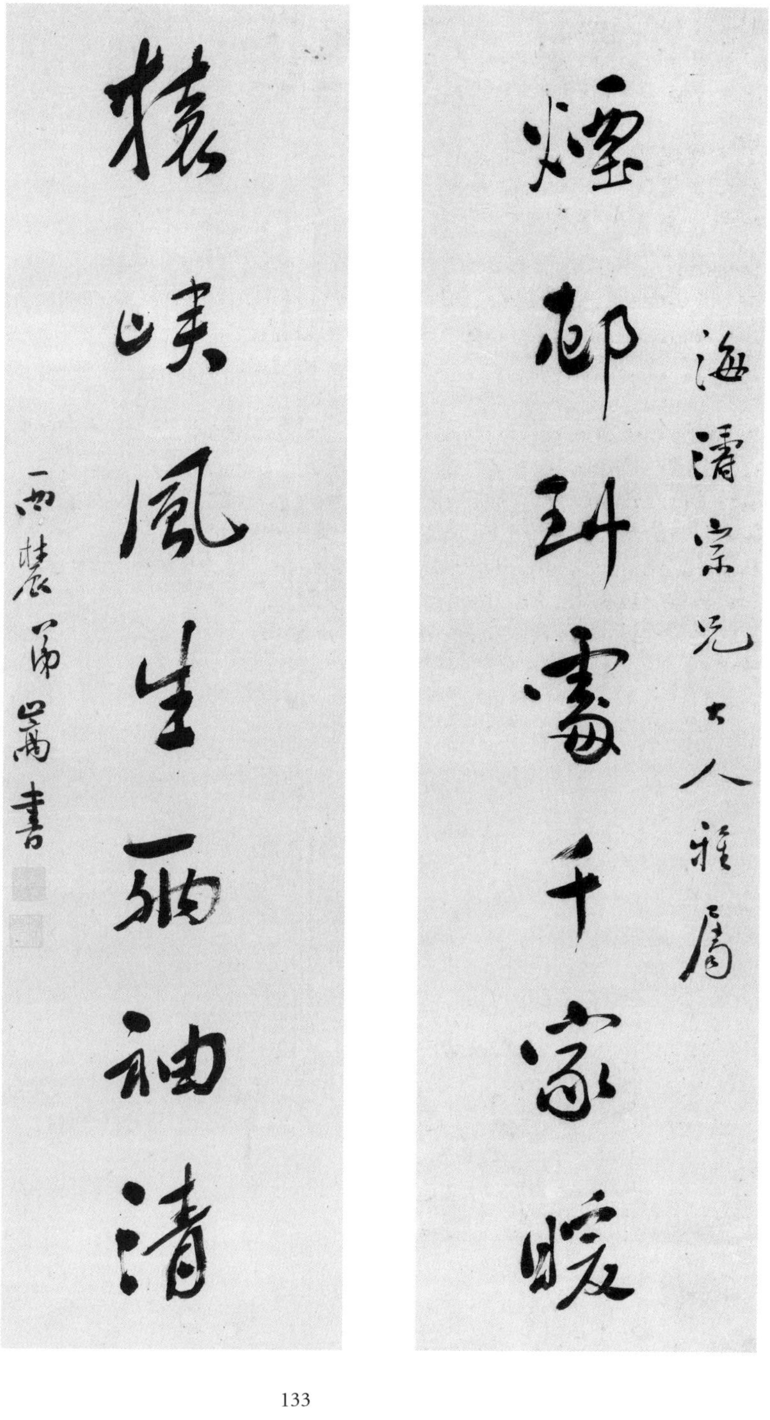
海清宗兄大人雅屬
猿峽風生兩袖清
書

44 **OU Weibai** 區爲柏 (c late 19th – early 20th centuries)

Couplet in regular script 楷書集《九成宮醴泉銘》七言聯

pair of hanging scrolls; ink on paper, 39.9 x 205.5 each 310.2003.a-b

蓱旨醴甘，冰凝鏡澈；道隨時泰，慶與泉流。
款識：焯生仁兄先生雅正。集九成宮醴泉銘。弟新甫區爲柏。
鈐印：區爲柏印。新甫。

Both duckweed and spring are sweet and pleasant; the water is as serene as ice, and as bright as a mirror. The Way flourishes as time moves on; fortune flows along with the river.

Inscription and signature: For appraisal of Mr Zhuosheng. Assembling words from the *Commemorative stele for the Sweet Spring at Jiucheng Palace.* Ou Weibai, alias Xinfu.

Kaishu (regular script) was the predominant script in the Tang dynasty. Among others, the scripts of Yan Zhenqing and Ouyang Xun (557–641), both leading officials at the court, were most valued. Their calligraphy has been noted for solidity and strength, reflecting their irreproachable moral character. Throughout history, their scripts have served as the foremost models of regular script.

The *Commemorative stele for the Sweet Spring at Jiucheng Palace* is one of the most recommended works in Ouyang calligraphic style, and is known for its sense of order and structure. It displays gracefulness while maintaining solemnity.

The life of Ou Weibai remains a mystery.

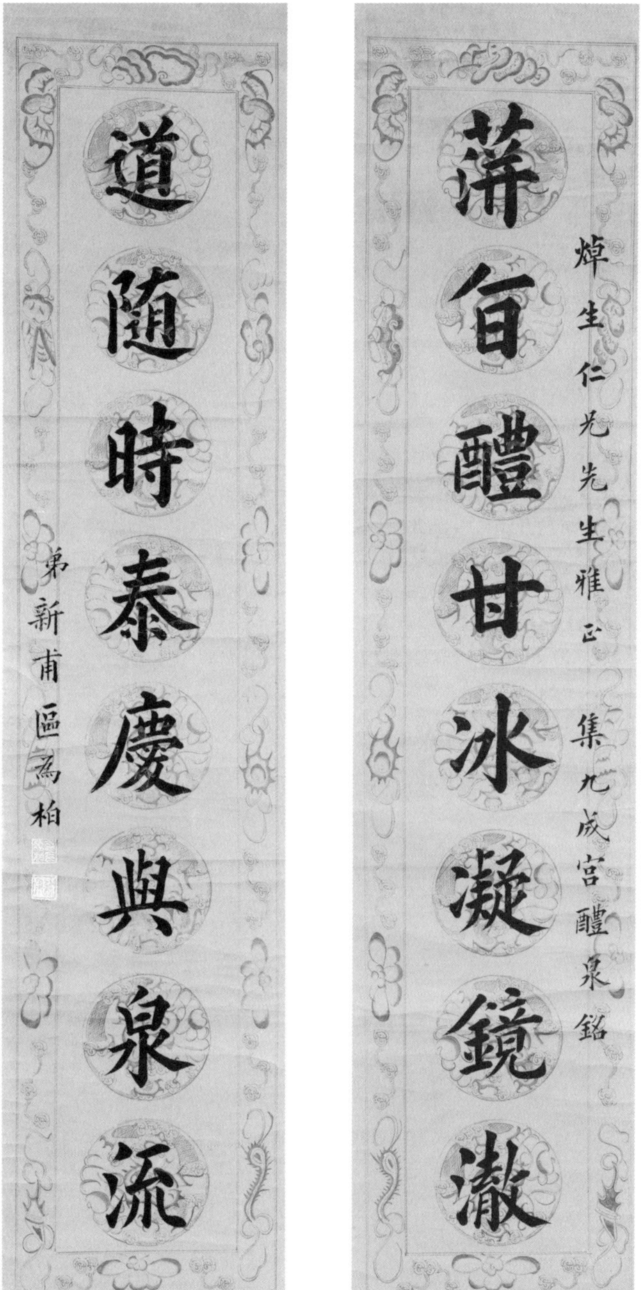
焯生仁兄先生雅正
萍旨醴甘冰凝鏡澈
集九成宮醴泉銘
道隨時泰慶與泉流
弟新甫區為柏

45 **HE Ruolin** 何若鏻 (Qing dynasty)

Couplet in running script 行書七言聯

pair of hanging scrolls; ink on paper, 33.2 x 180 cm each 309.2003.a-b

黃雞紫蟹堪攜酒，寶馬鳴珂曉蹋塵。
款識：和甫尊兄大人雅正。弟何若鏻。
鈐印：何若鏻印。展生。

Yellow chicken and purple crab should be savoured along with wine-drinking;
The precious horse jingled, treading on dust in the morning.

Inscription and signature: Written for the appraisal of respective Mr Hefu. He Ruolin.

Although the first line of the couplet was directly taken from a poem by the Qing dynasty poet Wu Weiye (1609–71), the image of the yellow chicken, crab and wine is ubiquitous in Chinese literature and is closely associated with the Chongyang or Double Nine Festival, which took place on the ninth day of the ninth moon. Customarily, this is the day for outdoor activities: climbing mountains, enjoying autumn scenery and picnics (chicken, crab and wine being favourite items for consumption). The expression of 'precious horse' and 'jingling patents' are symbols of illustrious and noble status. So the couplet expresses the unfettered lofty mood of the scholar-official, in which one experiences a temporary transformation from the life of a bureaucrat, to one who has cast aside the pressures of materialism in everyday life to enjoy nature's simplicity and purity.

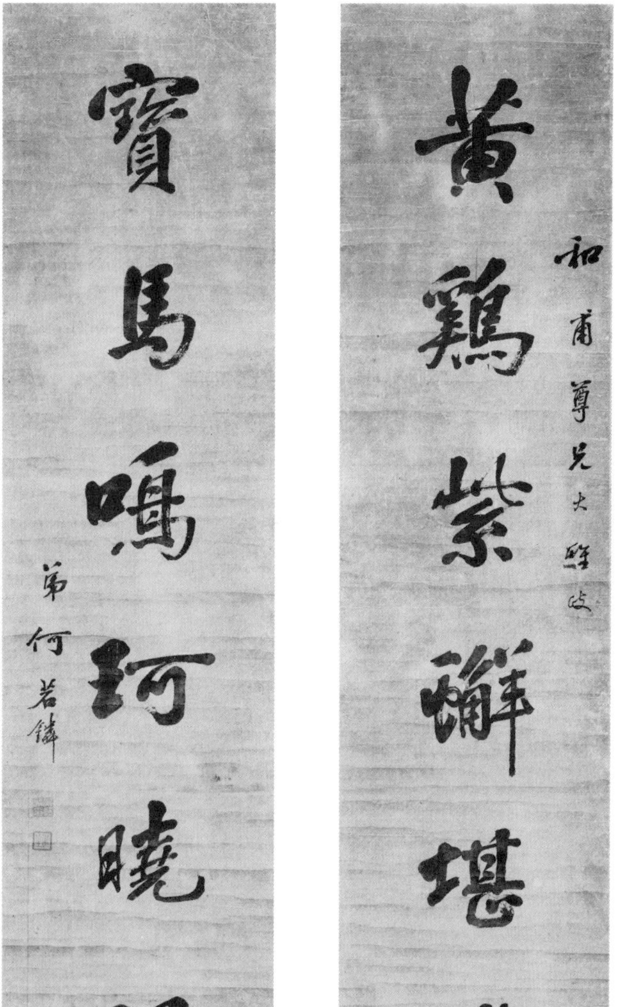
黃鷄紫蟹堪攜酒
和甫尊兄大雅政
寶馬鳴珂曉蹋塵
弟何若鏞

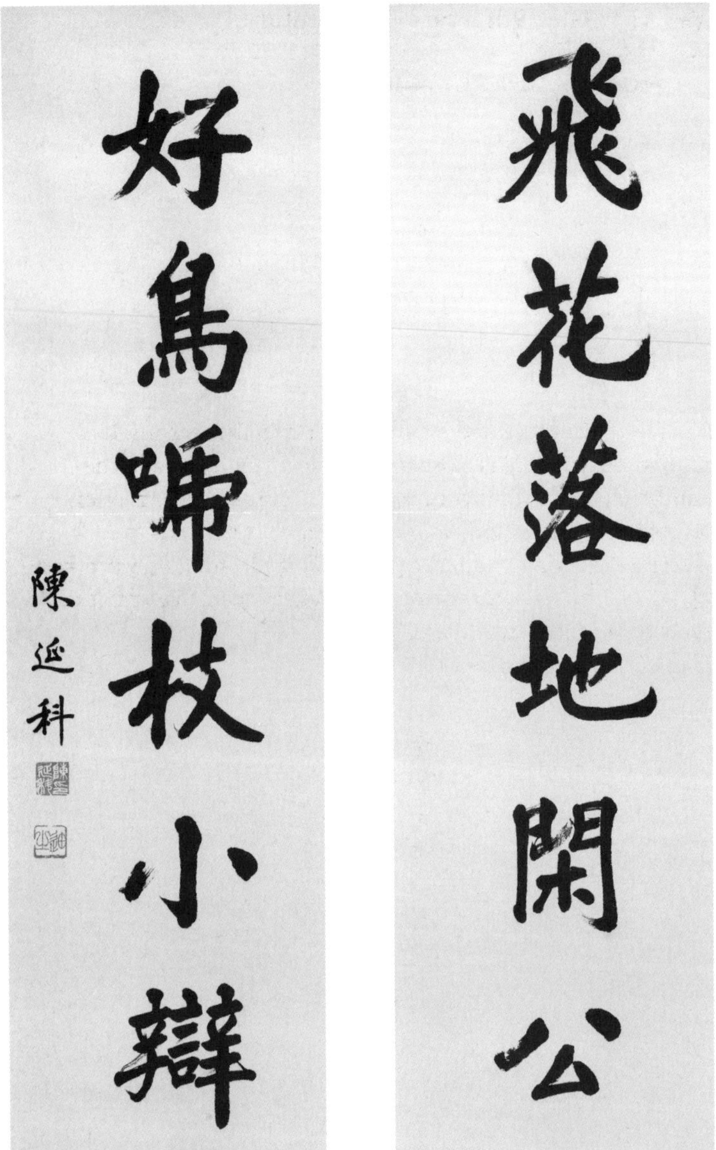
飛花落地閒公案
好鳥啼枝小辯才
陳延科

46 **CHEN Yanke** 陳延科 (c late 19th – early 20th centuries)

Couplet in regular script 楷書七言聯

pair of hanging scrolls; ink on paper, 137.2 x 32.7cm each 305.2003.a-b

飛花落地閒公案；好鳥啼枝小辯才。
款識：陳延科。
鈐印：陳延科印。迪之。

The falling of flowers onto earth is a carefree incident;
On the branches, the singing birds are also adept at talk.

Inscription and signature: Chen Yanke.

In a witty way, the couplet extols nature and expresses joy with the seasons. It is written in *kaishu* (regular script), and is close to the style of Ou Dayuan. The characters are square and architectural, showing a proper, compact construction of the *kaishu* style. During the Qing period, *kaishu* was not only a means to seek imperial favour, it became an exacting 'chancellery style', a model for all government documents. Students who aspired to government office started learning with Tang models of *kaishu* script, as reflected in this piece.

The life of Chen Yanke is unknown.

47 **Anonymous** 佚名

Couplet in cursive script 草書七言聯

pair of hanging scrolls; ink on paper, 35.5 x 165.1 cm each 296.2003.a-b

浮生若夢誰非寄，到處能安即是家。

The floating life resembles a dream; who is not a sojourner?
Thus everywhere would be home if one could settle.

These lines may be one of the most encountered couplets in Chinese Buddhist temples. They are seen, for instance, at Tuixingan Nunnery 退省庵 in West Lake, Hangzhou; at Ziguosi Temple 資國寺 in Fuding, Fujian; and at the Tianningsi Temple 天寧寺 in Leizhou, Guangdong. The popularity of the couplet demonstrates the firm hold in the minds of Chinese Buddhist adepts, that reality is fantasy and illusion and that life is a dream. The idea thrived in part because it found further philosophical support in Daoism. The Daoists believed that there is no definitive dividing line between reality and dream. What one considered real is often precariously dream-like. In *Zhuangzi*, the author recounts that he once dreamt himself to be a fluttering butterfly. When he woke up, he stumbled on whether he had dreamt he was a butterfly or a butterfly had dreamed he was Zhuangzi! Therefore, the acceptance that life is a dream is considered enlightenment, allowing people to free themselves from the ordinary cares of being.

The couplet, written by an anonymous calligrapher in unrestrained cursive script, is a perfect example of Chinese calligraphic art that reaches a harmonious balance between form and content.

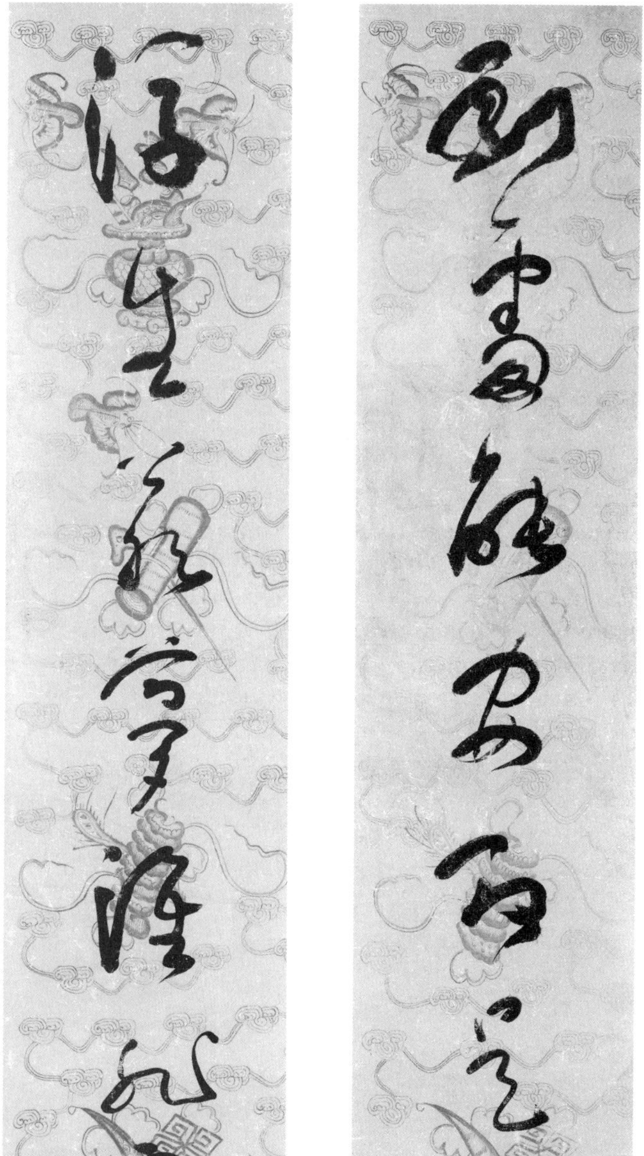

JAMES HAYES COLLECTION IN THE HOOVER INSTITUTION

CHEN Gongyin 陳恭尹 (1631–1700)
'Comments on calligraphy' in clerical script 隸書論書 handscroll; ink on paper

SU Er 蘇珥 (1699–1767)
Two poems of the Tang dynasty in cursive script 草書唐應制詩二首
hanging scroll; ink on paper

LI Jian 黎簡 (1747–1799)
Poem in cursive script 草書詩一首
hanging scroll; ink on paper

FENG Minchang 馮敏昌 (1747–1807)
'Comments on longevity' in running script 行書論壽文 hanging scroll; ink on paper

SONG Xiang 宋湘 (1756–1826)
Couplet in running-cursive script 行草八言聯 pair of hanging scrolls; ink on paper

HUANG Danshu 黃丹書 (1757–1808)
Couplet in running-cursive script 行草五言聯 pair of hanging scrolls; ink on paper

Mi Fu's poem in cursive script 草書米芾七絕《吳江垂虹亭作》
hanging scroll; ink on paper

WU Rongguang 吳榮光 (1773–1843)
Huang Tingjian's 'A poem for Yueyun' 臨黃庭堅《寄嶽雲帖》
hanging scroll; ink on paper

HUANG Peifang 黃培芳 (1779–1859)
'Comments on calligraphy' in cursive script 草書論書 handscroll; ink on paper

ZHANG Weiping 張維屏 (1780–1859)
Couplet in running script 行書八言聯
pair of hanging scrolls; ink on paper

Couplet in running script 行書七言聯
pair of hanging scrolls; ink on paper

PENG Tailai 彭泰來 (1790–1866)
Citation of texts by Xunzi, Xiahou Zhan, Fan Ye and Liu Ling
草書荀子、夏侯湛、範曄、劉伶文
four hanging scrolls; ink on paper

Couplet in clerical script 隸書七言聯
pair of hanging scrolls; ink on paper

ZENG Wangyan 曾望顏 (1790–1870)
Su Shi's poem in running-cursive script
行草蘇軾《書王定國所藏煙江疊嶂圖》
handscroll; ink on paper

Couplet in running script 行書五言聯
pair of hanging scrolls; ink on paper

ZENG Wangyan 曾望顏 (1790–1870), 孫奎耀 (*jinshi* 1811) 等 and others
Paintings and poems in running-cursive script 行草詩畫
pair of hanging scrolls; ink on paper

LUO Bingzhang 駱秉章 (1793–1867)
Couplet in running script 行書七言聯
pair of hanging scrolls; ink on paper

HUANG Zigao 黃子高 (1794–1839)
Couplet in seal script 篆書七言聯
pair of hanging scrolls; ink on paper

BAO Jun 鮑俊 (1797–1851)
Couplet in running-cursive script 行草八言聯 pair of hanging scrolls; ink on paper

Couplet in running script 行書八言聯
pair of hanging scrolls; ink on paper

Couplet in running script 行書八言聯
pair of hanging scrolls; ink on paper

LUO Tianchi 羅天池 (1805–?)
Couplet in regular script 楷書七言聯
pair of hanging scrolls; ink on paper

Shu Shi's 'A letter to an official at Huizhou'
行書臨東坡《與惠州都監書》
fan; ink on paper

ZHU Ciqi 朱次琦 (1807–1881)
Couplet in running-cursive script 行草七言聯 pair of hanging scrolls; ink on paper

LONG Yuanxi 龍元僖 (1810–1884)
Couplet in running-regular script
行楷八言聯
pair of hanging scrolls; ink on paper

LUO Dunyan 羅惇衍(1814–1874)
Couplet in running script 行草七言聯
pair of hanging scrolls; ink on paper

CHEN Pu 陳璞 (1820–1887)
Couplet in running script 行書七言聯
pair of hanging scrolls; ink on paper

Couplet in running script 行書八言聯
pair of hanging scrolls; ink on paper

FENG Yuji 馮譽驥 (1822– after 1883)
Sun Guoting's 'Preface to the Calligraphy Manual' 楷書孫過庭《書譜序》
four hanging scrolls; ink on paper

HUANG Huaisen 黃槐森 (1829–1902)
'Comments on phonology' in running script
行書論音韻學 hanging scroll; ink on paper

Couplet in running script 行書七言聯
pair of hanging scrolls; ink on paper

LIANG Yaoshu 梁耀樞 (1832–1888)
Couplet in running script 行書七言聯
pair of hanging scrolls; ink on paper

LI Wentian 李文田 (1834–1895)
Couplet in running script 行書七言聯
pair of hanging scrolls; ink on paper

Couplet in running script 行書七言聯
pair of hanging scrolls; ink on paper

DAI Hongci 戴鴻慈 (1853–1910)
Couplet in running-regular script
行楷八言聯
pair of hanging scrolls; ink on paper

CHEN Qikun 陳其錕 (*jinshi* 1826)
Couplet in running script 行書七言聯
pair of hanging scrolls; ink on paper

SU Tingkui 蘇廷魁 (1800–1878)
Du Fu's poem in cursive script 草書杜甫《戲題王宰畫山水圖歌》
fan; ink on paper

HUANG Lezhi 黃樂之 (*jinshi* Daoguang period 1821–50)
Couplet in clerical script 隸書七言聯
pair of hanging scrolls; ink on paper

DENG Chengxiu 鄧承修 (1841–1892)
Couplet in running script 行書五言聯
pair of hanging scrolls; ink on paper

PAN Yanyun 潘衍鋆 (*jinshi* 1862–74)
Ouyang Xiu's prose in cursive script
草書歐陽修《醉翁亭記》
hanging scroll; ink on paper

TANG Zongjun 譚宗浚 (1846–1888)
Couplet in running script 行書七言聯
pair of hanging scrolls; ink on paper

CHEN Botao 陳伯陶 (1855–1930)
Couplet in regular script 楷書七言聯
pair of hanging scrolls; ink on paper

WEN Su 溫肅 (1878–1939)
Couplet in running script 行書八言聯
pair of hanging scrolls; ink on paper

LIU Guanglian 劉光廉 (*juren* Guangxu period 1875–1908)
Couplet in cursive script 草書七言聯
pair of hanging scrolls; ink on paper

CHEN Ziqing 陳子清 (?–1946)
Couplet in regular script 楷書八言聯
pair of hanging scrolls; ink on paper

This collection of Qing scholar-officials' calligraphies, entirely from the Guangdong province, has been held by the Hoover Institution at Stanford University, California since 1989–90.

SUGGESTED READING

Bai, Qianshen. *Fu Shan's world: the transformation of Chinese calligraphy in the seventeenth century*, Harvard University Asia Center, Cambridge, Mass 2003

Barnhart, Richard M et al. *The Jade Studio: masterpieces of Ming and Qing painting and calligraphy from the Wong Nan-p'ing Collection*, Yale University Art Gallery, New Haven 1994

Billeter, Jean François. *The Chinese art of writing*, (trans Jean Marie Clarke & Michael Taylor), Skira, Geneva 1990

Boltz, William G. *The origin and early development of the Chinese writing system*, American Oriental Series 78, American Oriental Society, New Haven 1994

Bush, Susan & Murck, F Christian (eds). *Theories of the arts in China*, Princeton University Press, Princeton 1983

Capon, Edmund & Pang, Mae Anna. *Chinese paintings of the Ming and Qing dynasties*, International Cultural Corporation of Australia Ltd, Sydney 1981

Chang, Leon Lung-yien & Miller, Peter. *Four thousand years of Chinese calligraphy*, University of Chicago Press, Chicago/London 1990

Chaves, Jonathan. 'The legacy of Ts'ang Chieh: the written word as magic', *Oriental Art*, 23, 110. 2, summer 1977, pp 200–15

Cheng, François. *Chinese poetic writing* (trans Donald A Riggs & Jerome P Seaton), Indiana University Press, Bloomington 1982

Chiang, Yee. *Chinese calligraphy: an introduction to its aesthetics and technique*, 3rd edn (rev), Harvard University Press, Cambridge, Mass 1979

Clunas, Craig. *Elegant debts: the social art of Wen Zhengming*, Reaktion Books Ltd, London 2004

Cong, Wenjun, et al. *Zhongguo shufa shi* (history of Chinese calligraphy), 7 vols, Jiangsu jiaoyu Press, Nanjing 1999

Ellsworth, Robert Hatfield. *Later Chinese painting and calligraphy* 1800–1950, 3 vols, Random House, New York 1987

Fong, Wen C. *Beyond representation: Chinese painting and calligraphy, 8th–14th century*, Metropolitan Museum of Art, New York and Yale University Press, New Haven/London 1992

Fong, Wen C. et al. *Images of the mind: selections from the Edward L Elliott Family and John B Elliott Collections of Chinese calligraphy and painting at the art museum, Princeton University*, The Art Museum, Princeton University, Princeton 1984

Fu, Shen C F, et al. *Traces of the brush: studies in Chinese calligraphy*, Yale University Art Gallery, New Haven 1977

Goepper, Roger. 'Methods for a formal analysis of Chinese calligraphy, taking Sun Kuo-t'ing's Shu-p'u as an example' in *Proceedings of the International Colloquium on Chinese Art History 1991: painting and calligraphy*, part 2, National Palace Museum, Taipei 1992, pp 599–626

Goldberg, Stephen J. 'Court calligraphy of the early T'ang dynasty', *Artibus Asiae* 49, no 3/4, 1988-89, pp 189–327

Harrist, Robert E jr & Fong, Wen C. *The embodied image: Chinese calligraphy from the John B Elliott Collection*, The Art Museum, Princeton University, Princeton 2000

Hay, John. 'The human body as a microcosmic source of macrocosmic values in calligraphy' in Bush & Murck, *Theories of the Arts in China*, pp 74–102.

Ho, Wai-kam (ed). *The century of Tung Ch'i-ch'ang 1555–1636* (exhib cat), 2 vols, Nelson-Atkins Museum of Art, Kansas City, Mo 1992

Hummel, W Arthur (ed). *Eminent Chinese of the Ch'ing period*, United States Government Printing Office, Washington 1943

Ke, Shaomin, et al. *Qing shigao* (history of the Qing dynasty), Zhonghua Press, Beijing 1977

Kraus, Richard Curt. *Brushes with power: modern politics and the Chinese art of calligraphy*, University of California Press, Berkeley, Los Angeles, Oxford 1991

Kuo, Jason C & Sturman, Peter C (eds). *Double beauty: Qing dynasty couplets from the Lechangzai Xuan Collection*, The Chinese University of Hong Kong Art Museum, Hong Kong 2003

Ledderose, Lothar. *Mi Fu and the classical tradition of Chinese calligraphy*, Princeton University Press, Princeton 1979

Ledderose, Lothar. 'Some Taoist elements in the calligraphy of the Six Dynasties', *T'oung Pao* 70, nos 4–5, 1984, pp 246–78

Lee, Sherman E & Ho, Wai-kam. *Chinese art under the Mongols: the Yuan dynasty (1279–1368)*, The Cleveland Museum of Art, Cleveland 1968

Lin, Yajie (ed). *Guangdong lidai shufa tulu* (a catalogue of calligraphy in Guangdong throughout history), Guangdong Renmin Press, Guangzhou 2004

Lin, Yajie & Zhu, Wanzhang. *Ling'nan shuxue yanjiu* (Study on the calligraphy in Ling'nan reigon), Guangdong Renmin Press, Guangzhou 2004

Little, Stephen. 'Chinese calligraphy', *Bulletin of the Cleveland Museum of Art*, 74, no 9, Nov 1987, pp 372–403

Liu, Cary Y, Ching, Dora C Y & Smith, Judith G. *Character and context in Chinese calligraphy*, The Art Museum, Princeton University, Princeton 1999

Liu, Heng. *Zhongguo shufa shi: Qingdai juan* (history of Chinese calligraphy: Qing dynasty), Jiangsu Jiaoyu Press, Nanjing 1999

Liu, Yang & Capon, Edmund. *Fragrant space: Chinese flower and bird painting of the Ming and Qing dynasties from the Guangdong Provincial Museum*, Art Gallery of New South Wales, Sydney 2000

Liu, Yang. *Fantastic mountains: Chinese landscape painting from the Shanghai Museum*, Art Gallery of New South Wales, Sydney 2004

Lu, Fusheng et al (eds). *Zhongguo shuhua quanshu* (anthology of Chinese writings on painting and calligraphy), 14 vols, Shanghai shuhua, Shanghai, 1993–99

Manguel, Alberto. *The history of reading*, Viking Press, New York 1996

Martin, Henry-Jean. *The history and power of writing* (trans Ladia G Cochrane), University of Chicago Press, Chicago/London 1994.

McNair, Amy. *The upright brush: Yan Zhenqing's calligraphy and Song literati politics*, University of Hawaii Press, Honolulu 1998

Murck, Alfreda & Fong, Wen C. *Words and images: Chinese poetry, calligraphy and painting*, The Metropolitan Museum of Art, New York & Princeton University Press, Princeton 1991

Nakata, Yōjiro. *Chinese calligraphy: a history of the art of China* (trans Jeffrey Hunter), Weatherhill & Tankosha, New York/Tokyo/Kyoto 1982

Sturman, Peter. *Mi Fu: style and the art of calligraphy in Northern Song China*, Yale University Press, New Haven, Conn 1997

Sullivan, Michael. *The three perfections: Chinese painting, poetry and calligraphy*, The Walter Neurath Memorial Lectures, Thames & Hudson, London 1974

Tsang, Gerard C C et al. *Guangdong calligraphy*, Hong Kong Museum of Art, Hong Kong 1981

Tseng, Yuho. *A history of Chinese calligraphy*. Chinese University Press, Hong Kong 1993

Watt, James C Y & Li, Chu-tsing (eds). *The Chinese scholar's studio: artistic life in the late Ming period*, The Asia Society Galleries, New York 1987

Weng, Wango. *Chinese painting and calligraphy: a pictorial survey*, Dover Publications, Inc, New York 1978

Willetts, William. *Chinese calligraphy: its history and aesthetic motivation*, Oxford University Press, Oxford 1981

Zhu, Wanzhang (ed). *Guangdong chuanshi shuji zhijianlu* (records of extant calligraphic works from Guangdong), Tianjing Renmin Meishu Press, Tianjing 2003

INDEX OF ARTISTS